Highlights in American History:
1850 to the Present

Middle and Upper Grades

by
Grace Kachaturoff

Frank Schaffer Publications®

Author: Grace Kachaturoff
Cover Artist: Ralph Hashoian

Frank Schaffer Publications®

Send all inquiries to:
Frank Schaffer Publications
3195 Wilson Drive NW
Grand Rapids, Michigan 49544

Highlights in American History: 1850 to the Present—middle and upper grades

ISBN: 0-86734-787-2

3 4 5 6 7 8 9 10 11 MAZ 10 09 08 07 06 05

TABLE OF CONTENTS

INTRODUCTION

"History is . . . the record of what one age finds worthy of note in another."
Jakob Burckhardt

This book is the second in a series, *Highlights in American History*. The first book concentrates on the beginnings of our nation through the 1850s. This book treats the events in our nation's history from 1850 to the present day. History provides the content and the means for studying about ourselves and others. It is the story of people and includes stories and insight into our heritage—stories which end happily and stories which end tragically. The stories are about heroes and heroines, exciting adventures, explorations, wars, ideas, and change. The goal of this book is to develop more student interest and enthusiasm in social studies and to bring historical understandings and insights to the existing social studies' curriculum. It is the intent of the author to help students understand why things happened the way they did and why the study of history has many uses. The knowledge of our heritage is essential in the making of effective, contributing American citizens. History has much to offer that can help students to achieve an understanding of world society and to develop ways of resolving its problems.

The format of this publication is similar to that of the first book. Each unit is introduced by a two-to three-page explanatory discussion of significant ideas and principles of a specific period of time. The explanations are brief, enriching and reinforcing the information presented in the United States' history textbooks. Student activity sheets follow the explanatory discussions. The activities are designed to promote attainment of historical objectives—knowledge, skills, attitudes, and values. The instructional objectives will challenge students to think critically—to comprehend, to analyze, to synthesize, and to value as they interact with the content of history. Each unit culminates with a number of carefully designed suggestions for teaching strategies. These suggestions are intended to be widely applicable so that teachers may modify and adapt them to better suit the learning techniques of their students. The teaching strategies encourage independent and group work, as well as work to be accomplished cooperatively by the entire class. Often, data is presented for the teacher which may be shared with students in developing a particular strategy.

Studying history should be a broadening, diversifying activity that helps students comprehend current happenings and enriches human decision-making. One of the purposes of studying history is to help students read newspapers to acquire a greater understanding of the situations in which they find themselves in the world today. Students should have the understandings and skills to define the roles they should assume and to see the forces of change and resistance that surround them on every side. Marc Bloch, defining history as being the study of men in time, analyzed the many laudatory uses of history, such as helping people to live better and understanding the present by the past and the past by the present. He also firmly believed, even if history were judged incapable of any use, "its entertainment values would remain in its favor."

CHANGE AND DISCORD BEFORE THE CIVIL WAR

Many Americans believed the adoption by Congress of the Compromise of 1850 would bring about an end to the sectional disputes among the states over slavery. Many Americans were optimistic that this "great compromise" would settle the issue of slavery forever. The status of slavery was now determined for every territory and area controlled by the U. S. government between the Atlantic and Pacific Oceans.

In the northern states it was, nevertheless, difficult for people to accept the new Fugitive Slave Act, one of the provisions of the compromise. This act was even more stringent than it had been previously. At many public meetings, people loudly declared their refusal to obey the provisions of the fugitive slave law. For several years the northern abolitionists had been conducting the "underground railroad" to help escaped slaves gain their freedom. The new law of 1850, if strictly enforced, would close every station on the underground railroad. Harriet Beecher Stowe's book *Uncle Tom's Cabin*, published in 1852, dramatically describes how good and innocent blacks were mistreated in the South. After reading the book, Northerners were even more willing to help escaped slaves gain their freedom.

In 1852 Franklin Pierce, a Democrat from New Hampshire, won the presidency. In his inaugural address, he stated that he hoped the sectional disputes would not threaten the economic prosperity of the country. Men in business and in industry were elated with these words. They wanted Congress to spend more time attending to the business interests of the country rather than to the sectional disputes over slavery. Signs of increasing prosperity and wealth were apparent. Huge deposits of gold and silver were discovered in California. Acres and acres of wheat fields could be seen in the fertile soils of Wisconsin, Iowa, and Minnesota. More products were being manufactured in the mills and factories in the North, giving people jobs. The finished products were shipped to world markets. The merchant marine fleet was increasing. During the 1850s there were 16,500 miles of new railroads laid. Many of the large cities and ports were now connected, and trade expanded between the Great Lakes and the Atlantic coast and throughout the states and territories.

Americans were moving westward. People who were restless and ambitious moved into the undeveloped territories in the West. Railroads, roads, trails, steamboats, canals, and other means of transportation helped to encourage adventuresome homesteaders to begin the trek westward for better economic opportunities. Communication was revolutionized as telegraph wires were installed.

"King Cotton" in the South appeared to be sharing in this growth and prosperity. Thousands of acres of cotton were planted. In fact, the South neglected to develop any other form of industry because of the endless demand for cotton by the mills in the North and in Europe. The South, therefore, depended more and more on slaves to work in the cotton fields. Some sugar and rice crops were also cultivated in the South.

During the 1850s immigration to America continued to increase. Laborers were needed in the factories and mills in the growing American cities. Various forms of distress in foreign countries such as war, famine, rebellion, and religious persecution aided in encouraging immigrants to come to America, a land of plenty and a refuge of democracy. Irish immigrants generally remained in the cities on the Atlantic coast and worked in the factories and mills. German immigrants tended to settle in the agricultural and rural regions. Many Chinese laborers immigrated to the Pacific coast.

During the early 1800s, the percentage of white children enrolled in school increased. A few religious groups organized schools for blacks in the North. It was illegal to teach black children and adults reading and writing although, in a few instances, they were provided with instruction. A few slaves taught themselves to read and write. During the 1850s more schooling was demanded. In most urban areas the percentage of foreign-born had increased considerably. Many Americans argued for more schooling to eliminate foreign influences and to indoctrinate the newcomers to the American way of life. They also believed that school reform and economic prosperity were directly related. Certain developments made it possible to support reforms in education. Improvements in the technology of printing made textbooks available and relatively inexpensive. Young women were recruited as teachers at very low wages. In many instances they were paid less than half of what male teachers made. School reformers favored schooling for all white children with public financial support and control.

Problems as well as prosperity and wealth accompanied the new technological developments, growth in the economy, and dramatic increases in population. Americans began thinking differently about their values and their changing institutions as more railroads, factories, and faster ships were being built. The arts flourished during these years before the Civil War. Herman Melville published *Moby Dick*, a story about the sea, and Stephen Foster wrote the song, "Old Folks at Home." *Uncle Tom's Cabin* was produced as a stage play. Walt Whitman published *Leaves of Grass*. He is now regarded as the first American poet of world stature. Reforms in other areas were apparent. Elizabeth Cady Stanton appeared before the legislature in New York to promote the cause of women's suffrage. New religious groups were formed. Experiments in group living were established. Trade with Japan was opened.

Congress had used compromises to help our nation grow and strengthen. However, the Compromise of 1850 did not maintain a peaceable settlement between the North and the South. Northerners and Southerners found themselves growing further apart. Fighting occurred in Kansas over the slavery issue. The North was angered by the provisions of the Fugitive Slave Act. The Dred Scott decision further embittered the North when the Supreme Court ruled that Dred Scott, a slave from Missouri, was not to be regarded as a free man, but as property. After the election of Abraham Lincoln as president of the United States, John Brown raided Harpers Ferry for guns which he planned to give to slaves to fight against their masters. He was found guilty of murder and treason and hung. In spite of the Compromise of 1850, war between the states now appeared imminent.

In 1861 the southern states decided to leave the Union and form another nation, the Confederate States of America. Each state in the Confederacy had the right to have slaves. Jefferson Davis was selected to be the first president of the Confederate States. He wanted the United States government to order all its troops to leave the South. When the Union soldiers refused to leave Fort Sumter, Confederate soldiers were ordered to open fire. The war between the states—the Civil War—had begun.

IDENTIFYING MAJOR EVENTS

Identify the year the following events occurred. Then, briefly identify the event and discuss how it created discord among the states which eventually led to the Civil War.

YEAR

_____1. Compromise of 1850 is enacted. _____

_____

_____

_____

_____2. Harriet B. Stowe publishes *Uncle Tom's Cabin.* _____

_____

_____

_____

_____3. The Kansas-Nebraska Act is passed. _____

_____

_____

_____

_____4. Supreme Court hands down Dred Scott decision. _____

_____

_____

_____

_____5. Lincoln-Douglas debates take place. _____

_____

_____

_____

_____6. John Brown's raid on Harpers Ferry occurs. _____

_____

_____

_____

_____7. Lincoln is elected president. _____

_____

_____

_____

Name_____

MAP STUDY

On an outline map of the United States, identify the states included in the United States in 1860. Then, note whether they are free or slave states.

Answer the following questions:

1. Which territories were open to slavery under the Compromise of 1850?

_____

_____

2. Which territories were open to slavery under the Kansas-Nebraska Act?

_____

_____

SUGGESTED TEACHING ACTIVITIES

1. Topics for further study:

   a. Brigham Young
   b. slavery
   c. abolition movement
   d. "the Little Giant"
   e. Underground Railroad
   f. John Brown's raid

   g. California gold rush
   h. Harriet Tubman
   i. "bleeding Kansas"
   j. Dred Scott
   k. Lincoln-Douglas debates
   l. Oregon Trail

   m. Walt Whitman
   n. Harriet Beecher Stowe
   o. Stephen Foster
   p. Herman Melville
   q. Elizabeth Cady Stanton
   r. Fort Sumter

2. Assign student volunteers to read Harriet Beecher Stowe's *Uncle Tom's Cabin* and to produce a videotape of selected dramatized scenes from the book to present to their classmates. How was this book received when it was first published? Why? How did it promote the cause of the North?

3. Assign students to make a chart listing the territories under control of the United States in 1860. List the year of acquisition, previous owner, how acquired, and the states that were eventually formed from the region.

4. Assign students to prepare a chart showing all the presidents who served during the 1850s, their positions regarding slavery, and at least one important decision each made regarding the slavery issue during his administration.

5. Plan a field trip for the class to an art museum to see paintings and other art objects from the 1850s. Assign students to identify one that is appealing to them and tell (orally or in written form) how it is related to the historical period and why they selected it. Student volunteers may wish to make a report to the class on "1848-1861: From Sea to Shining Sea" from *The U.S.A.: A History in Art* by Bradley Smith. (New York: A Gemini Smith Inc., Book — Doubleday & Company, Inc., 1975).

6. Student volunteers may present a concert to the class which includes Stephen Foster's music and other musical compositions from the 1850s.

7. Oral Presentations: Have students imagine one of the following situations and prepare a short speech to present to their classmates, using the suggested questions.

   a. They are asked by John Brown to participate in the raid at Harpers Ferry. Will they join the raiders? Why or why not?

   b. They are in the audience during one of the Lincoln-Douglas debates. How did Lincoln impress them? Why? How did Douglas impress them? Why? For whom would they have voted? Why?

8. Assign students to write a short paper describing how Eli Whitney's cotton gin works and how it affected the economy in the South. They may wish to mention how life in the South may have been different if Eli Whitney had not invented the cotton gin.

THE INEVITABLE WAR OF REBELLION

The attack on Fort Sumter began the war of rebellion between the states. The next day, on April 14, 1861, President Abraham Lincoln called on the states in the Union for 75,000 troops to suppress the rebellious states. Northerners and Southerners believed that their causes were righteous and that victory would be theirs within a few weeks. The South would fight for independence and the North for the reestablishment of the Union.

In 1861 the resources for war in the North and in the South were unequally matched for the years of fighting ahead. Resources such as troops, wealth, weapons, industries, telegraph lines, and transportation lines in the North far exceeded those in the South. More people lived in the North than in the South. Large cities existed in the North; very few were to be found in the South. Immigrants were helping to increase the population rapidly in the North. The North was in a state of change, becoming more industrialized and diverse in its economy. Farm machinery was available in the North to free men to serve in the army. However, Southerners were solely dependent upon cotton for their wealth, and this required the use of slaves. Manufacturing was almost non-existent in the South. More people were illiterate in the South than in the North.

It is noteworthy that millions of people in the South who had no slaves nor interest in slavery fought bravely for the South because they believed that the North meant to subjugate them and to turn their lands over to the blacks. The South also believed that it had military advantages because the fighting would be done on its own land, that its men were better trained soldiers and officers, that other states would soon join the South, and that the Democrats in the North would provide support for them. None of these "hopes" became reality. Another major advantage of the South was the fact that its people understood why they were fighting. They wanted to be left alone and to be independent. The war aims in the North were not as specific and as easy to understand.
Even before the northern troops were organized, it was decided to move on to Richmond, the capital of the Confederacy in July, 1861. The Northerners, under General Irvin McDowell's command, suffered disaster at Manassas, a small town near Bull Run Creek, about 35 miles southwest of Washington, D. C.

In 1861 a blockade had been established by the North, forcing cotton exports to drop dramatically. The British did not militarily intervene on behalf of the South. This, of course, weakened the South economically and militarily. The North was victorious in a naval battle involving the *Monitor*, a small iron craft, shaped like a torpedo, against the South's *Merrimack*. The *Merrimack* was made "ironclad" after its sunken hull was raised. This ship could be described as a "floating fort."

In the war in the West, the battles were mainly fought by the North for control of the Mississippi River which would provide it political and economic advantages. This would free an outlet for commerce among the northwestern states and sever ties between the Confederacy and the states of Arkansas, Louisiana, and Texas. General Ulysses S. Grant and Admiral David G. Farragut were the major Union leaders in these battles. General Grant's forces took Fort Henry and Fort Donelson on the Tennessee and Cumberland Rivers. Then, they fought the battle of Shiloh victoriously against General Albert S. Johnston, one of the most outstanding leaders in the Confederate army. In a spectacular battle, Admiral Farragut captured New Orleans.

The Union army in the East was outwitted and outfought by the Confederate forces. In the second battle at Bull Run in August 1862, the Union forces again retreated. General McClellan was able to stop General Robert E. Lee's invasion of Maryland at Sharpsburg on the Antietam Creek. However, General McClellan, again, did not crush the enemy so that the Confederate army was able to get back across the Potomac to Virginia soil. When the bloodiest single day's battle of the war was fought at Antietam Creek, President Abraham Lincoln issued his famous Emancipation Proclamation. This Proclamation freed slaves in all states that did not belong to the Union. "All persons held as slaves in any State in rebellion against the United States, shall be then, thenceforward, and forever free."

The Battle of Gettysburg, fought in July 1863, was the most important battle of the war. This was also the only one fought on northern territory. General Lee was forced to withdraw by the third day of battle. The South had lost 28,000 soldiers and the North had 23,000 casualties. At the same time General Grant was able to take Vicksburg. These were terrible losses for the South.

General Sherman, in 1864, advanced from Chattanooga to Atlanta which surrendered to the northern forces after several battles. General Grant finally reached the capital of the South, Richmond. As the Union forces marched into the city of Richmond, General Robert E. Lee surrendered at Appomattox Court House in Virginia. The war between the states was finally over and the Union was preserved. By the end of 1865, the Union was also entirely slave free.

With the fall of Richmond and the surrender of General Robert E. Lee's army, the Confederacy collapsed, utterly devastated. When the Civil War ended in 1865, nearly 600,000 Americans had died. The men and women in the South had defended their cause with admiration. Most important, the war determined that the United States would remain a single nation.

THE MATCHING GAME

Match the phrase in column 1 with its
description in column 2.

COLUMN 1

_____1. Jefferson Davis

_____2. Dorothea D. Lynde Dix

_____3. General Robert E. Lee

_____4. Battle at Antietam

_____5. Emancipation Proclamation

_____6. Admiral David G. Farragut

_____7. "Anaconda Plan"

_____8. Monitor

_____9. General William T. Sherman

_____10. General George B. McClellan

_____11. Clara Barton

_____12. General Ulysses S. Grant

COLUMN 2

a. After defeating the Confederate fleet in the Gulf of Mexico, he captured the city of New Orleans. In another battle, he is credited with saying, "Damn the torpedoes! Full speed ahead!"

b. He served as president of the Confederacy.

c. She served under the surgeon general and helped to organize a women's nursing corps.

d. After setting fire and devastating the city of Atlanta, he marched his troops to the sea.

e. He attended West Point and fought in the Mexican War. As commander, he maintained high standards of readiness for his Union troops.

f. This established the fact that the war was fought to preserve the Union and to eliminate slavery.

g. His most impressive victory was in the campaign for Vicksburg.

h. For the troops of the North and South, this battle was the worst single day of the war.

i. An ironclad ship, it helped to reinforce the Union's blockade of southern ports.

j. He surrendered his troops to northern forces at the Appomattox Court House.

k. This was developed by the commander of the Union army to blockade the South and to take control of New Orleans and the Mississippi River, thus bringing victory to the North.

l. She volunteered to nurse the wounded troops and, in 1877, founded the American Red Cross.

COMMANDERS OF THE NORTH AND SOUTH

1. Write a short biographical sketch of General Ulysses S. Grant.

_____

_____

_____

_____

_____

_____

_____

_____

2. Write a short biographical sketch of General Robert E. Lee.

_____

_____

_____

_____

_____

_____

_____

_____

3. How do these two men compare as outstanding military leaders?

_____

_____

_____

_____

_____

_____

_____

SUGGESTED TEACHING ACTIVITIES

1. Topics for further study:
   a. "Stonewall" Jackson
   b. Emancipation Proclamation
   c. U. S. Military Academy
   d. changing role of women
   e. weaponry in Civil War
   f. changing military strategy
   g. Fort Sumter
   h. Clara Barton
   i. Dorothea Dix
   j. Belle Boyd
   k. "Anaconda Plan"
   l. Pickett's Charge
   m. Gettysburg Address
   n. "ironclad" ships
   o. Admiral David Farragut
   p. President Abraham Lincoln
   q. President Jefferson Davis
   r. communication

2. Assign students to prepare a graph using the following information. What inferences can they make by studying the graph? How has medical help changed since the Civil War? Why did so many soldiers die in the Civil War?

War	Number of Men Engaged	Number of Casualties
Civil War	2,213,363	643,392
Spanish-American War	306,760	4,108
World War I	4,734,991	320,518
World War II	16,112,566	176,245
Korean War	5,720,000	157,530
Vietnam War	8,744,000	211,438

3. Industrialization was already deeply rooted in the North when the Civil War began. Assign students to write a short paper about one of the following industries: coal production, railroads, farm machinery, communications, clothing, or food processing. How did the industry develop and why? How did it improve the quality of life during the 1860s?

4. Share with your class the article entitled "The Odyssey of Pvt. Rosetta Wakeman, Union Army" by Eugene L. Meyer (*Smithsonian*, January 1994). This is an extraordinary account of women who fought in the Civil War and about a court case which involved a woman who played the role of a soldier in an enactment of the Civil War. Also, a special issue published by American Heritage, *Civil War Chronicles* (1992), has a number of very interesting articles about Lincoln and an Italian freedom fighter, Robert E. Lee, warships, and Samuel Colt.

5. As a class make arrangements to see the film or videotape entitled *Gettysburg*. Class discussion can involve topics, such as military decision making, military strategies, weapons, or the life of a soldier. Also, Ken Burns' *The Civil War Series*, videotapes are excellent. The nine episodes are available from PBS, Alexandria, VA (1990).

Suggestions for Supplementary Reading:

Beatty, Patricia, and Phillip Robbins. *Eben Tyne: Powdermonkey*. New York: Morrow Junior Books, 1990.
Catton, Bruce. *The American Heritage Picture History: The Civil War*. New York: American Heritage Publishing Co., Inc./Bonanza Books, 1960.

PEACEMAKING PROBLEMS AFTER THE CIVIL WAR

Although slavery was the cause of the Civil War, both the North and the South believed that it was not. The South insisted that it was fighting for its constitutional rights that were being denied by the North. The North, on the other hand, insisted that it took up arms not to free the slaves but to preserve the Union. Lincoln's Emancipation Proclamation that freed the slaves was issued during the war.

During the war the leaders in the North debated on how to handle the "peace" after the war. Little agreement existed concerning what should become of the freed slaves and how political and economic powers were to be restored in the South. According to Lincoln's plan, he expected all states to abolish slavery. He would pardon almost all Southerners. When one tenth of the citizens of a state who voted in the 1860 presidential election took a solemn oath to support the United States Constitution, he would admit that state and let the people rule themselves as they had before the Civil War. Many in Congress did not agree with this plan, especially the Republican members known as "Radicals." They felt it was the responsibility of Congress, not the president, to draw up a plan for reconstruction. They feared that the plantation owners and Confederate leaders would try to keep the slaves under their control if the plan were too lenient. The Radical congressmen wrote their own reconstruction bill that was spiteful and harsh, and President Lincoln vetoed it.

The slaves were not prepared for their freedom. Often, they were homeless, jobless, without food and clothing. In March 1865, Congress established the Freedman's Bureau to help them and poor southern whites. With limited resources, they found jobs and homes for them and provided medical care and food. They established schools and hospitals. The Southerners did not support the work of the bureau because they felt threatened. They also believed that education would encourage the blacks to become independent and demand opportunities and guaranteed rights.

With the surrender of General Robert E. Lee's army on April 9, 1865, the Confederacy collapsed in spite of the bravery and courage of the Southerners during the war. On the evening of April 14, President Abraham Lincoln attended Ford's Theater with his wife and two guests. John Wilkes Booth, a southern sympathizer and actor, stepped into the president's box and shot him in the back of the head. The president was carried, unconscious, to a home across the street from the theater and medical aid was given. Nevertheless, early the next morning, President Abraham Lincoln died. Booth was caught in a barn and shot after the barn had been set on fire.

A few hours after Lincoln's assassination, Andrew Johnson of Tennessee took the oath of office as president of the United States. He was born in North Carolina; his father died when he was very young. His mother had to work to support the family. He never attended school and became a tailor's apprentice. When he married, his wife taught him to read and write. He was an ambitious man who took part in government and became known as an honest and loyal champion for the working man and for the Union.

In 1865, while Congress was in recess, President Johnson tried to apply Lincoln's plan with a few changes to the southern states. He appointed governors and ordered the states to frame new constitutions, which they did. State officers were elected, legislatures were chosen, and the Thirteenth Amendment was accepted. In December 1865, all the states except Texas had met the terms President Johnson had set. Congress, however, refused to recognize these states. Reconstruction was their responsibility, not the president's. Congress did not approve of former military leaders and known southern sympathizers being elected to political office. Furthermore, they refused to recognize the states because they had passed the Black Codes that guaranteed control over the blacks. If black men were found to be unemployed, they were fined. If they could not pay the fine, they could be hired out to private employers, often their former masters. Blacks were restricted to jobs on the farm or doing housework. They could not vote, serve on juries, nor go to school with whites. These codes brought about a new form of black slavery.

Congress believed that President Johnson was responsible for the Black Codes and for permitting former southern sympathizers to be elected to office. President Johnson was offended and refused to compromise. Congress tried unsuccessfully to pass a number of acts for reconstruction. The president vetoed them. Congress, eventually, passed the Civil Rights Act and a new Freedmen's Bureau bill over his veto. Congress submitted the Fourteenth Amendment to the Constitution. This amendment declared all persons born or naturalized in the United States were citizens and could not be denied the right to vote.

Congress finally passed the Reconstruction Act of 1867 that divided the South into five military districts, each under command of a major general of the Union Army. To return to the Union, the states had to rewrite their basic constitutional laws, and they had to allow all adult men, black and white, to vote for delegates. The new constitutions had to guarantee voting rights to blacks and the states had to ratify the Fourteenth Amendment. Lastly, Confederate leaders were denied the right to vote or hold office. By 1868 seven more states were readmitted to the Union. The last three states to be admitted also had to accept the Fifteenth Amendment. This declared that the right of the citizen to vote shall not be denied or abridged by any federal or state governments on account of race, color, or previous condition of servitude.

The black registered voters outnumbered the white voters in many of the states. This frightened many white Southerners who distrusted the black citizens. Blacks were elected as representatives to Congress and held jobs in state and local governments. Southern whites were threatened by the growing political power of the blacks. The "grandfather clause" began to appear in state constitutions that said that if a man's grandfather had not voted, that man could not vote either. Violent action was taken by the Ku Klux Klan, an organization that threatened and terrorized freed blacks, especially those who might vote. They murdered and beat blacks, burned homes and churches, and broke up meetings held by blacks.

Some Northerners went South to help educate the freed slaves; others went as government officials who used their power to impoverish the South and make money for themselves. These people became known as *carpetbaggers*. *Scalawags* were also unpopular in the South. They were Southerners who sympathized with the North. It was difficult for people with such differing views to work together in changing the southern governments.

Since it was difficult for freed slaves to get land, a system of sharecropping developed. Blacks rented land from plantation owners. They paid the rent by giving the landowner part of the crops harvested at the end of the growing season. Very few blacks were able to become successful at sharecropping since the plots were very small and often the soil was poor. Nevertheless, they kept a few animals, grew a garden, and were able to call the farm their own.

The Tenure of Office Act was passed by Congress in 1867 which forbade the president to dismiss civil officials, including members of his own cabinet, without the consent of the Senate. President Johnson suspended Secretary of War Edwin M. Stanton, who was sympathetic with the Radical Republicans. Congress failed to impeach President Johnson by a single Senate vote. The president finished his term. General U. S. Grant succeeded him as president in 1869.

The blacks had won their freedom and some important legal and constitutional guarantees. However, they had no commitment from the government to enforce these guarantees. In reality, the racial issue was left unresolved, to be confronted by others in the years ahead.

MAKING CONNECTIONS

Draw connections between the terms in column 1 and their descriptions in column 2 by placing the correct letter on the blank.

COLUMN 1

_____1. Radical Republicans

_____2. sharecroppers

_____3. Thirteenth Amendment

_____4. impeachment

_____5. Klu Klux Klan

_____6. Thaddeus Stevens

_____7. scalawags

_____8. Abraham Lincoln

_____9. The Freedmen's Bureau

_____10. Fourteenth Amendment

_____11. veto

_____12. carpetbaggers

_____13. Tenure of Office Act

_____14. Fifteenth Amendment

COLUMN 2

a. This organization helped blacks in the transition from slavery to freedom.

b. This document forbids slavery in the United States.

c. When Congress passes a bill and the president does not like it, he returns it to Congress unsigned. The bill does not become law.

d. This document gave black males the right to vote.

e. This charge occurs when a public official is brought to trial for a wrongdoing such as "treason, bribery, or other high crimes and misdemeanors."

f. These congressmen wanted to punish the Confederate states by making the terms of readmission harsh.

g. This law prevents the president from dismissing a person in his cabinet without the permission of the Senate.

h. This organization set out to keep blacks from voting, to punish scalawags, and to drive carpetbaggers from the South by violent means.

i. They were Southerners who sympathized with the North in believing that slaves should be free and enjoy the rights and privileges guaranteed to all Americans.

j. This document declared that no state could take away citizens' rights without due process of law.

k. He was a leader of the Radical Republicans and a bitter enemy of the South.

l. These people rented land and paid the rent with a certain percentage of their harvest each year.

m. Many Northerners went south to acquire wealth and power.

n. He was the first president to be assassinated in office.

"IFFY" QUESTIONS

Support your position by presenting at least two reasons.

1. If you had been president following President Lincoln's administration, what kind of a reconstruction plan for the South would you have developed? Why? What are the strengths of your plan? The weaknesses?

_____

_____

_____

_____

_____

_____

2. If you were a member of Congress in 1867, would you have insisted that Confederate leaders and southern sympathizers be denied the opportunity to vote and to hold political office? Why or why not?

_____

_____

_____

_____

3. If you were a member of Congress in 1868, would you have voted to impeach President Johnson? Why or why not?

_____

_____

_____

VOTING RIGHTS

SUGGESTED TEACHING ACTIVITIES

1. Topics for further study:
   a. Abraham Lincoln
   b. Freedmen's Bureau
   c. Frederick Douglass
   d. Edwin M. Stanton
   e. Thaddeus Stevens
   f. Andrew Johnson
   g. John Wilkes Booth
   h. impeachment
   i. scalawags
   j. carpetbaggers
   k. grandfather clause
   l. Ku Klux Klan
   m. Thirteenth Amendment
   n. Fourteenth Amendment
   o. Fifteenth Amendment

2. During the Reconstruction period 16 blacks were elected to Congress. Blacks used their recently granted right to vote and elected blacks to serve in Congress. Senators Hiram Revels and B. K. Pruce and Representatives Benjamin Turner, Josiah T. Walls, Joseph Rainey, Robert Smalls, Jefferson Long, and John R. Lynch were a few. Have student volunteers select at least one of these leaders and describe who he was, what kind of person he was, his educational background, and what contribution he made to our country.

3. Have students imagine that they were living in Atlanta, Georgia, or Charleston, South Carolina, shortly after the war. Write a letter to a friend describing what life in your city is like with the federal troops, scalawags, and carpetbaggers.

4. Walt Whitman, a great American poet, wrote a famous poem about the death of President Abraham Lincoln in which he compares the United States to a ship and assigns President Lincoln as its captain. Distribute copies of the poem "O Captain! My Captain!" to each student. Have students read the poem together (a choral reading) or individually. Students can discuss poetry as a means of communication and also the effectiveness of using metaphors. What kind of pictures are brought to mind as you read the poem? What kind of emotions do you feel as you read the poem? What were the accomplishments of the "captain"? Of President Lincoln?

5. Assign students to read "I Have a Dream" by Martin Luther King, Jr. These words were spoken by Martin Luther King, Jr., in 1963. Review the Thirteenth, Fourteenth, and Fifteenth Amendments to the Constitution made during the Reconstruction period. Are there any connections between the amendments and this speech? Explain. Could this speech be described as one of hope and determination? Why? What is King's vision for all Americans?

Year	Population of the United States	Slave Population
1790	3,929,214	697,624
1800	5,308,483	893,602
1810	7,239,881	1,191,362
1820	9,638,453	1,538,022
1830	12,866,020	2,009,043
1840	17,069,453	2,487,355
1850	23,191,876	3,204,313
1860	31,443,321	3,953,760
1870	39,818,449	

6. Prepare a graph showing the population of the United States and the Slave Population: What were the implications of these numbers in terms of the reconstruction plans?

RECONSTRUCTION COMES TO AN END

As a soldier General Ulysses S. Grant demonstrated compassion, courage, and intelligent military strategy, but as a statesman he was incompetent and untrained. He knew very little about politics and the administration of public office. He had been rewarded for his greatness in war by being elected president of the United States. He was so honest, direct, and innocent himself that he failed to understand the fraud, corruption, and deceitfulness being committed by public officials. Politicians in Congress took advantage of him. When he had accepted the surrender of General Robert E. Lee, he had demonstrated generosity and understanding. However, within a few months in office he viewed the problem of reconstructing the South in narrow and harsh terms, just like the Radical Republicans.

The unsettled conditions during and after the Civil War provided an opportunity for dishonesty. Many people grew wealthy as they participated in criminal or fraudulent schemes. State and local governments fell into the hands of dishonest groups of people or rings. "Boss" Tweed robbed the city of New York of millions of dollars before he was imprisoned in 1878. Secretary of War William W. Belknap resigned to escape impeachment for sharing the criminally obtained money from the dishonest management of army posts in the West. Even President Grant's private secretary was implicated in frauds which robbed the government of its tax on whiskey. Western stagecoach lines and corrupt post office officials made false returns of the amount of business done along their routes. They secured large amounts of money from Congress for carrying the mails. Some "pet routes" cost the government thousands of dollars annually and carried fewer than a dozen letters a week. Congressmen accepted large amounts of railroad stock as presents from railroad officials who wanted government favors for their companies.

Before the end of President Grant's first term of office, Carl Schurz, Charles Francis Adams, and George Curtis began a reform movement. They advocated civil service reform. This meant that appointments to public office should be made on the basis of qualification or merit and not on political pull of the candidates. Second, they wanted the tariff or taxes on certain commodities to be reduced. Lastly, they wanted the Federal troops in the South to be withdrawn. The reform party nominated Horace Greeley as a candidate to challenge President Grant in his bid for a second term. Greeley's defeat was overwhelming.

It was fortunate for the United States that two able and competent men served at the head of the State Department. When the government of Russia asked the United States to buy Alaska,

Secretary of State William H. Seward, serving under President Johnson, accepted the offer and paid Russia $7,200,000 for 577,390 square miles of land. Later, he annexed the Midway Islands, just west of Hawaii, to the United States. Secretary of State Hamilton Fish, serving under President Grant, kept the United States from going to war against Spain over the execution of nine American citizens in 1873.

Napoleon III, Emperor of France, thought that this might be the time to expand French interests in Mexico since the Americans were involved in Civil War. He appointed an "emperor" to accept the "throne of Mexico" and sent an army of 35,000 Frenchmen to protect his lands. When the Civil War was over, Secretary of State William H. Seward put pressure on France to get out. In 1865 American troops were sent to the Mexican border. Napoleon III immediately withdrew his troops from Mexico. The Mexicans captured, court-martialed, and shot Napoleon III's appointed emperor. During the Civil War, the British allowed warships built for the Confederacy to leave the ports of England to go after and prey upon Union ships. They destroyed some $20,000,000 worth of merchant ships and cargoes. The British also encouraged the Confederate cause, lengthening the war for many months. A committee of statesmen, agreed upon by Hamilton Fish and the English, decided that Great Britain had been guilty and awarded the United States damages of $15,500,000 in gold.

Even though the war left the South impoverished, it served to encourage business in the North. Factories employed more men and production increased in northern cities and towns. People migrated westward to mines and ranches. Several projects were approved by Congress to build railroads to the Pacific, and the Homestead Act of 1862 encouraged pioneers to cultivate a farm for five years—and then it would be theirs.

Directors of the Union Pacific Railroad formed a construction company called the Credit Mobilier. As directors they awarded themselves huge building contracts at enormous profits. To secure favors from Congress and to avoid investigation of their dishonest activities, they distributed shares of the Credit Mobilier stock where they would do the most good in helping them operate dishonestly. Even honest men accepted the stock without investigating its origin.

The rapid expansion of business brought on a severe economic panic in 1873, causing the cost of living to rise extremely high for the working classes. Strikes occurred and labor meetings demanded an eight-hour day, government inspection of mines and factories, and the exclusion of Chinese laborers from the United States. Reform leaders and movements demanded direct issue of money by the government, an end of land grants to railroads or corporations, the regulation of railroad rates, a tax on incomes, and the establishment of the Department of Labor in Washington, D.C.

General Rutherford B. Hayes, governor of Ohio, was nominated as candidate for president and the Democrats nominated Governor Samuel J. Tilden of New York. This election was the most exciting in American history. There was a question of the legality of the votes. As a compromise an Electoral Commission was created by Congress. This commission declared Hayes president, just a few days before Inauguration Day.

With the recovery from the panic of 1873, the industries in the United States began a period of great expansion. New inventions such as the electric light, telephone, phonograph, bicycle, typewriter, and elevated railroad gave the necessary push to better economic times. Cities grew in population.

In spite of personal unpopularity, President Hayes gave the country one of the most courageous and honest administrations in its history. He immediately withdrew federal troops from the South, and this signaled the end of reconstruction. Furthermore, he dismissed important political leaders in the Republican party and sent a commission to China to begin negotiations of a treaty to protect workers on the Pacific Coast. He also worked to improve the living conditions of the American Indians. After a few months in office, a railroad strike occurred, and he called upon the militia of several states to end the disorder.

President Hayes was probably deserving of a second term, but his party nominated James A. Garfield, a reformer, for the presidency and Chester A. Arthur was selected as his running mate. Arthur then supported a strong party by giving government jobs to party members who, then, would have to contribute money to the party. Garfield was elected president. As president he was uncompromising: two senators resigned their seats in the Senate.

A few weeks after the resignation of the senators, as President Garfield entered the Baltimore and Potomac railroad station at Washington, a fanatic, Charles Guitreau, shot the president in the back to rid the nation of a "traitor" and to put Arthur into the presidency. President Garfield died after a few weeks of suffering in September 1881.

GETTING THE "SCOOP"

Assume you were a reporter for your local newspaper when each of the "stories" listed below occurred. Write an article for your newspaper, selecting any two of the events. Your articles should include headlines and answer the following questions: Who was involved? What happened? When did it happen? Where did it happened? Why did it happen? How did it happen?

EVENTS:
A. The Election of President Rutherford B. Hayes
B. The Purchase of Alaska
C. The Removal of Troops from the South
D. The Assassination of James A. Garfield

I. Article One:

_____

_____

_____

_____

_____

_____

_____

_____

_____

II. Article Two:

_____

_____

_____

_____

_____

_____

_____

_____

_____

"JIM CROW" LAWS

When the federal troops were withdrawn from the South, the states began to enact the "Jim Crow" laws. This term, "Jim Crow," was taken from the name of a popular minstrel show character, a black crow, named Jim. The crow was a character in a song and dance act which insulted and made fun of slaves. The minstrel shows were performed by white actors who darkened their faces.

The name "Jim Crow" began to be used to describe black people, and they did not like it. When the blacks were freed, the term was used to describe unfair laws which were passed by the states which limited the rights of former slaves.

Examples of "Jim Crow" laws:
1. All voters had to pay a two-dollar poll tax (a voting tax) when they registered to vote.
2. Voters had to pass a test to prove their ability to read and understand documents such as the state and federal constitutions or the Declaration of Independence to register.
3. Voters were required to own land or property to register.
4. Blacks were denied the use of public parks, beaches, and picnic areas.
5. Blacks and whites could not go to school together.

1. What were the purposes of these laws?

   _____

   _____

2. Do you think these laws were fair? Why or why not? Note that the first four laws above do not refer to race.

   _____

   _____

   _____

3. Did anyone oppose these laws? Explain.

   _____

   _____

   _____

4. Which law do you think was the most unfair? Explain.

   _____

   _____

   _____

   _____

   _____

SUGGESTED TEACHING ACTIVITIES

1. Topics for further study:
   a. President Ulysses S. Grant
   b. Radical Republicans
   c. "Boss" Tweed
   d. "half-breeds" and "stalwarts"
   e. Ku Klux Klan
   f. Seward's Folly
   g. Hamilton Fish
   h. Union Pacific Railroad
   i. Credit Mobilier
   j. "Jim Crow" laws
   k. President R. B. Hayes
   l. Election of 1876
   m. President James Garfield
   n. Horace Greeley
   o. "Lemonade Lucy"

2. Assign students to prepare a graph using the following information:

School Enrollment Rates Per 100 Population, by Sex and Race: 1850-1920			
Year	Blacks and Other Races	Whites	Total
1850	1.8	56.2	47.2
1860	1.9	59.6	50.6
1870	9.9	54.4	48.4
1880	33.8	62.0	57.8
1890	32.9	57.9	54.3
1900	31.1	53.6	50.5
1910	44.8	61.3	59.2
1920	53.5	65.7	64.3

Class Discussion: What inferences can you make from the graph you have prepared regarding school enrollment of whites? Of blacks? What factors may have brought about the increases? When did the increases occur and why? What do you think the data for the 1990s would look like? Why?

3. Prepare a time line, using the following events:
   a. General Ulysses S. Grant becomes president of the United States.
   b. President James A. Garfield is assassinated.
   c. Federal troops are removed from the South.
   d. The United States purchases Alaska.
   e. "Boss" Tweed is imprisoned.
   f. The Homestead Act is passed.
   g. Thirteenth Amendment to the United States Constitution is ratified.
   h. Fourteenth Amendment to the United States Constitution is ratified.
   i. Freedmen's Bureau is established.
   j. The Ku Klux Klan is formed in the South.
   k. Rutherford B. Hayes is elected president.

4. Assign students to imagine that their parents own a plantation in Georgia and that the 200 slaves who worked for them are now free. Students will then write a letter to a friend in New York City and tell that individual how they feel about the freed blacks and how they plan to manage the plantation.

5. Ask student volunteers to imagine that they are one of the four children of a slave family who are now freed. Tape-record how they feel about their newly won freedom and what their family plans are. Play the tape for the class and discuss some of the common problems confronted by all the freed slaves.

THE SOUTH AND CLOSING THE WESTERN FRONTIER

By the 1870s new businesses and industries were being developed in the South. Lumbering and iron and steel industries were established. Textile factories provided some jobs, but workers were soon in debt to factory owners who also owned the company stores that sold food and clothing to them. Industrialization in the South could not compete with the North, with its human and technological resources. The South continued to remain primarily a land of farms.

In the late 1860s cotton and tobacco production increased in the South. The southern planters refused to sell any land to blacks. They were forced to work as laborers on the farms and plantations. Plantation owners developed a system of farming called sharecropping. The plantation owners divided their land into small plots and allowed a black family to work the plot and then "share" the crop at harvesting time with them. Generally, the "share" was a certain percentage of the produce. Seeds for planting, fertilizer, and even food, clothing, and other supplies were available at the land owner's store, generally at high prices. When their portion of the crops was marketed, the sharecroppers found themselves heavily in debt for the supplies and food they had purchased in the land owner's store. It was difficult to make a living as a sharecropper. Very few sharecroppers were ever able to purchase land of their own.

Most white Southerners never accepted the idea of blacks as equal citizens. Blacks were denied many rights; even the Supreme Court declared that separate accommodations did not deprive blacks of equal rights. Violence, such as lynching, was used against the blacks to control them with terror and fear.

A black leader, Booker T. Washington, tried to improve opportunities for blacks by discouraging violence and conflict. He was a schoolteacher who eventually became the head of Tuskegee Institute which stressed agricultural, domestic, and mechanical training. He told blacks to work hard and to be honest and thrifty. He believed that blacks only needed to learn vocational skills to survive. It appeared that he did not want blacks to compete nor seek social equality with whites. He did not demand political and civil rights. To many blacks Washington's ideas would keep them in a position of permanent inferiority. On the other hand, William E. B. DuBois, the first black man ever to earn a doctorate degree at Harvard University, demanded human justice and guaranteed rights for all blacks. He told blacks to get the very best education they could and the doors of opportunity would be opened to them. The blacks were free, yet they were denied political power and opportunities to improve themselves through education. Poverty, racial prejudice, and oppression continued to face black Americans at the end of the nineteenth century.

Before the 1860s settlements had been made on the Pacific coast, in California, and in Oregon. After the 1860s stories about rich gold and silver deposits in the western areas attracted many miners eager to make money quickly. People in the East left their homes to stake out claims in Colorado, Nevada, and other states. Some people were lured westward by the short-grass pasture for cattle and sheep. Others were persuaded to go west because of the fertile prairie soil for farming. The completion of the transcontinental railroad lines helped encourage more settlement. The railroad companies brought in construction workers to help build the railroads that linked other western cities and towns. The Homestead Act of 1862 encouraged settlers to stake a claim to 160 acres of land if they would live on the land for five years. The railroad and steamship companies advertised these free lands in Europe; this enticed thousands of immigrants to make their homes on the Great Plains.

Americans, as they pushed westward, liked to think of the Great Plains as an area awaiting settlement. Thousands of Indians, some forcibly relocated there by the Americans, lived in the Great Plains already. The settlers never considered whether it was right to make their homes on lands that belonged to and were occupied by the Indians. Depending on the region where they lived, the Indians had developed their own way of life. The Southwest Indians were primarily farmers, growing corn in their irrigated fields. In that same region, some tribes lived nomadically by hunting, farming, and sheep herding.

Another large group, the Plains Indians, lived a nomadic life. They were hunters who were primarily dependent on the buffalo or bison for food, clothing, and shelter. These Indians were described as more powerful and often militant warriors. They fought many battles, some successful, against the advancing American settlers and armed forces. Nevertheless, they were finally defeated by the increasing numbers of American settlers and superior technology of the United States Army. The Plains Indians were forced to give up their lands and live on restricted reservations set up by the United States government which made life oppressive, demeaning, and poverty-stricken.

Buffalo Bill, William F. Cody, was hired by the railroad companies to kill bison; the animals were shot by tourists from the windows of their trains, for sport. The bison herds upon which the Indians depended for their livelihood were disappearing. By 1875 only a thousand or so buffalo remained and this brought about the end of the Plains Indians' way of life. Victories in battle were rare for the Indians. The settlers, supported by the United States Army, took over Indian lands for ranches, farms, roads, and mines. Indians such as Chief Joseph, Chief Crazy Horse, Chief Sitting Bull, and many others fought bravely to save their lands and their way of life, but defeat was inevitable. Thousands of Indians were killed in the battles of Little Big Horn and Wounded Knee Creek.

The United States government signed treaties with the Indians. Most of the treaties that were made gave the federal government Indian lands. In return, the Indians were promised certain rights and privileges. Sometimes, treaties were forced upon the Indians. Americans rarely kept their promises as stated in the treaties. Many Americans believed that the Indians would be better off if they became more like Americans. The Dawes Act was passed in 1887, forcing Indians to become farmers. What this act accomplished, though, was a greater loss of land for the Indians. The bison had disappeared from the plains, most of their lands were in the hands of the white settlers, and their culture was changed forever.

As connecting lines to the transcontinental railroad were constructed, cattle ranching became an important industry. The Great Plains offered an open range where herds of cattle could graze free of charge and unrestricted by the boundaries of private farms. This changed as more farmers settled in the Great Plains and cattle ranches were established with fenced-in grazing land. When the cattle were ready for market, they were taken on the long drive to a railroad station. The long drive began in the springtime when the calves were rounded up, branded, and driven by cowboys to a railroad station. The cowboys were veterans of the Confederate army, freed slaves, Northerners, Mexicans, and immigrants. They were usually assigned such jobs as wrangler or cook.

Farming on the Great Plains was difficult and risky. The period between 1865 and 1900 witnessed a tremendous expansion of agricultural facilities. As a consequence, a surplus of farm products existed in the United States, driving the prices down. The farmers thought that the railroads, charging high rates, were responsible for their problems since they depended on the railroads to take their products to market. The railroad companies also owned elevators and warehouses and charged high rates for the farmers to use these facilities. Farmers also felt that banks and insurance companies took advantage of them when they needed credit to purchase machines or to enlarge their land areas. Lastly, they felt they had no control over prices for their products which were sold on the competitive market nor did they have control over the prices they paid for goods and equipment they bought. The farmer and farming were an essential part of America. Now, industry was competing with the farmer as people left the farms to work in factories and shops in towns and cities.

PUTTING THINGS IN ORDER!

Arrange each set of events in chronological order, beginning with the first event in time as 1, the second as 2, etc.

SET I:

_____ A. Chief Geronimo is captured.

_____ B. The Battle of the Little Bighorn is fought.

_____ C. The Battle of Wounded Knee is fought.

_____ D. The Dawes Act is passed.

SET II:

_____ A. Federal troops are withdrawn from the South.

_____ B. General Ulysses S. Grant is elected president of the United States.

_____ C. The Union Pacific, the first transcontinental railroad, is completed.

_____ D. The Ku Klux Klan is organized in the South.

SET III:

_____ A. Nevada is admitted to the United States.

_____ B. The *Plessy v. Ferguson* decision of the Supreme Court upholds "separate but equal" racial facilities.

_____ C. North Dakota is admitted to the United States.

_____ D. The Homestead Act is passed.

SET IV:

_____ A. Colorado is admitted to the United States.

_____ B. The barbed wire fence is invented.

_____ C. Utah is admitted to the United States.

_____ D. Mark Twain publishes *The Adventures of Huckleberry Finn.*

SET V:

_____ A. Joel Chandler Harris publishes *Uncle Remus: His Songs and His Sayings.*

_____ B. The Dawes Act is passed.

_____ C. Rutherford B. Hayes is elected president of the United States.

_____ D. Nez Perce Indians resist relocation.

Set VI:

_____ A. The Homestead Act is passed.

_____ B. The Union Pacific, the first transcontinental railroad, is completed.

_____ C. The NAACP is founded.

_____ D. The Battle of Wounded Knee is fought.

HUNTERS OF THE PLAINS

Select one of the following Indian groups on which to prepare a cultural study: Cheyenne, Kiowa, Sioux, Apache, Nez Perce, Arapaho, Crow, or Blackfoot. The following questions may serve as a guide for the study.

a. Describe geographically — climate, natural resources, etc. — where they lived. Locate the area on an outline map of the United States.

b. Briefly tell about their historical background.

c. How did they provide food, clothing, and shelter for themselves?

d. What were the responsibilities of men, women, and children?

e. How were the children taught?

f. How did these people entertain themselves?

g. How did they govern themselves?

h. What kind of men and/or women were leaders? Why? Who were some of their important leaders?

i. How did they get along with people who were not members of their tribe?

j. Did the United States sign any treaties with this group? Explain.

Model for Studying Societies

Origins - - - - - Beginnings - - - - - [**Heritage**] - -The Past - - - Historical Consideration

Location - - - - Climate - - - [**Geographical Environment**] - - - - - - Natural Resources

[**People**] - - - - - - - Human Resources

[**Values**] - - - - - - - Goals, Ideals

[**Institutions**]

Education — **Creative Experiences Art, Music, Drama** — Family

Economy — Government — Religion

Resistance - - [**Contact With Other Societies**] - - -Conflict - - -Diffusion

[**Future**]

SUGGESTED TEACHING ACTIVITIES

1. Topics for further study:
   a. Battle at Wounded Knee
   b. Maggie Lena
   c. Booker T. Washington
   d. *Plessy v. Ferguson* case
   e. W. E. B. Du Bois
   f. Little Bighorn Battle
   g. Homestead Act
   h. mining towns
   i. Chief Geronimo
   j. Annie Oakley
   k. sharecropping
   l. Plains Indians
   m. George A. Custer
   n. Indian reservations
   o. Bureau of Indian Affairs
   p. Chief Black Kettle
   q. Chief Crazy Horse
   r. Chief Sitting Bull
   s. treaties
   t. NAACP
   u. Apaches
   v. cowboys
   w. Dawes Act
   x. Mark Twain

2. Assign students to prepare a chart comparing the Indians and the white settlers as to:
   a. property ownership
   b. family relationships
   c. bison
   d. treaties
   e. relationship to nature and environment
   f. war
   g. material possessions

   Discuss the similarities and differences in the two columns.

3. Assign each student to select one of the following statements and to write a short paper explaining his or her position.
   a. The inability of the Indians to unite against the white settlers and United States army led to their being driven out of their homes and lands.
   b. The Great Plains and/or far West were unpopulated and awaited settlement by American miners, farmers, and ranchers.

4. The bison was the main source of food for the Plains Indians. Food was only one of the many things that the bison contributed to the Plains Indians. Bison skin was used in many ways. In 1850 there were about 20 million bison on the Great Plains. By 1889 there were 551 left. Today there are about 15,000 bison which are located in fenced gamed preserves.
   Class Discussion: How did the Plains Indians use the bison? Who deprived the Indians of their main source of food? Why? When bison herds began to disappear, what happened to the hunters of the Plains?

5. Assign volunteers to create a mural showing all the people and activities occurring on the Great Plains between the 1850s and 1900s. Be certain to include hunters of the Plains, cattlemen, cowboys, miners, railroad construction workers, farmers, shopkeepers, and doctors. Display the mural and discuss the closing of the American frontier.

6. Read selected chapters orally to the students from *The American Cowboy* written and illustrated by Will James. The cowboy is taken through three generations, from the 1830s to the 1940s. The author tells the story, which moves quickly, in a detailed, eventful, and interesting manner.

Suggestions for Supplementary Reading:

Ashabranner, Brent. *To Live in Two Worlds: American Indian Youth Today.* New York: Dodd, Mead, & Company, 1984.

Holling, Holling C. *The Book of Cowboys.* New York: Platt & Munk, Publishers, 1962.

James, Will. *The American Cowboy.* New York: Charles Scribner's Sons, 1942.

LaFarge, Oliver. *A Pictorial History of the American Indian.* New York: Crown Publishers, Inc., 1956.

Malone, John Williams. *An Album of the American Cowboy.* New York: Franklin Watts, Inc., 1971.

EXPANSION INTO AN INDUSTRIAL ECONOMY

The United States became the first manufacturing nation in the world during the later 1800s. The national income from manufactured goods was far greater than the income from farm products. Many factors contributed to this industrial growth. Basic raw materials and energy resources such as coal, iron, timber, petroleum, and water power were plentiful. A large and growing population also provided a supply of laborers. People either moved from the farms to the cities or workers came from other countries. An increasing number of inventions also helped to bring about industrialization. Furthermore, there were men who were willing and eager to invest their energies and monies in business. They were sometimes known as "captains of industry" and "robber barons" who organized large-scale production and distributed the manufactured goods to markets. The markets were large because the population was growing. Railroads provided an inexpensive means of transporting raw materials to factories and finished products to markets.

The federal government promoted economic growth. With its help, the railroad trackage increased from 30,000 miles in 1860 to 193,000 miles in 1900. The government made public resources available to private companies on generous terms to encourage industrial growth. Congress passed protective tariffs against foreign competitors that greatly helped the American manufacturers to grow and expand.

New technologies and the discovery of new materials and productive processes were evident. From 1776 to 1860 only 36,000 patents were registered in the United States. From 1860 to 1890 nearly 440,000 patents were granted. Improvements in communication were necessary for expanding industries. The first transatlantic telegraph cable was laid to Europe. The telephone, typewriter, cash register, and calculating machines greatly aided in the expansion of business. The incandescent electric bulb and phonograph also contributed to industrial expansion. Thomas A. Edison introduced the laboratory, a workplace for developing new ideas and creating new inventions. Companies began to establish their own laboratories. Mass production and the moving assembly line were developed.

Another important technological invention was the development of steel. Iron was transformed into steel by blowing air through molten iron to burn out the impurities. Pittsburgh became the center of the steel industry. When Edwin L. Drake dug the first oil well in Pennsylvania, the petroleum industry began its extraordinary growth. Refrigerated freight cars, new ways of milling flour, and new methods of canning foods and condensing milk all had an impact on the industrial development in the United States. The radio, airplane, and automobile reshaped American social and cultural life. In 1895 there were four automobiles on the streets of the United States; by 1917 there were 5 million automobiles being driven by Americans.

The number of factories and companies in the United States began to increase rapidly during the 1870s and 1890s. Many Americans invested their own savings and got bank loans to start companies. Sometimes two or more persons pooled together their monies to begin a factory and shared in the profits of the company. By the end of the 1800s corporations, which were formed by obtaining charters or licenses from the state government to start specific businesses, were more common. Corporations could raise money by selling stocks, shares of the company, to members of the public. As businesses expanded rapidly, many people made money and grew tremendously wealthy such as Cornelius Vanderbilt, Andrew Carnegie, Leland Stanford, and Jay Gould. Not all of the wealthy families spent money on themselves only. A few of them gave generously to museums, universities, libraries, and other public institutions. The business leaders did not like competition. Some of them joined together to organize monopolies which gave them control of the market for their businesses. John D. Rockefeller, a leader in the oil business, formed one of the first monopolies in this country. Once a monopoly gained control, it caused the prices to rise and no one could do anything about it.

The American standard of living was rising significantly. At the same time, people felt that not enough of the profits of the companies were being passed on to their workers to create an adequate market for the goods they were producing. A growing resentment was developing as the gap between the wealthy and the poor was widening. About 1 percent of American families controlled 88 percent of the nation's industries.

Americans were moving from the farms into the cities, seeking better economic opportunities. Many factories employed European immigrants who almost doubled the nation's population between 1860 and 1890. Many of them came from southern and eastern European countries to escape poverty and oppression of their homelands. Men worked in the factories, but so did women and children. Factory owners increased their profits by hiring women and children to whom they paid very low wages. They worked long hours in dangerous and unhealthy workplaces. There was no job security and the factory tasks were routine, repetitive, and monotonous.

As the gap between workers and employers grew even wider, the workers wanted shorter working hours, better wages, and safer workplaces. Laborers tried different ways to solve their common problems. The "Molly Maguires" were organized by Pennsylvania miners. The railroad strike of 1877, a major labor conflict, brought in the federal troops and over 100 people died before the strike ended. The Knights of Labor disapproved of strikes and advocated an eight-hour day and the abolition of child labor. Against the advice of the leadership, some strikes were called, and membership in the Knights of Labor rapidly declined.

The American Federation of Labor, founded by Samuel Gompers, was an organization of many different trade unions. Unskilled workers and women were excluded from membership. Members wanted better wages and working conditions and an eight-hour work day. They felt their differences with the owners of the factories could be worked out in collective bargaining, that is, in a meeting where they would discuss their grievances. If necessary, they would call a strike, which meant they would stop working.

The American Federation of Labor called a general strike on May 1, 1886. Strikes and demonstrations took place all over the country. Strikers at the McCormick Harvester Company were harassed by the police. The strikers called a meeting at the Haymarket Square in Chicago to protest the murder of four workers the day before. While they were meeting, the police appeared and demanded that they leave. An unidentified person threw a bomb and killed seven policemen and injured many others. During the Haymarket Riot, the police fired into the crowd and killed four more people. Eight individuals who were anarchists (people who are against government of any kind) were charged with the murder of the policemen and all were found guilty in a trial that many thought was unfair. The individual who threw the bomb was not found.

A violent strike occurred at the Homestead plant of the Carnegie Steel Company in Pennsylvania. When the Company spokesman, Henry Clay Frick, announced more wage cuts for the workers, they decided to call a strike. He immediately shut down the plant and called the Pinkerton Agency to send 300 strikebreakers. The strikers attacked them and drove them away. The National Guard troops were called and the workers, defeated, returned to their jobs within a few months, accepting the low pay.

The Pullman Strike began during the winter of 1893-94 when the company reduced the wages of its workers by 25 percent. Federal troops were sent in when the strikebreakers and the workers clashed. Eugene V. Debs, one of the principal leaders of the American Railway Union, was imprisoned for six months.

The workers' unions emerged in a weakened state at the end of the century. The power and wealth of the owners of companies and corporations continued to grow. Union membership was low. Women, blacks, and unskilled workers were not invited to become members. Because unions used strikes that sometimes became violent to meet their goals, people thought they were dangerous. Since many of the workers were foreigners, some people thought that unions wanted to overthrow the American government. Workers were unable to create an organization to compete with the growing industrial power and wealth.

CONNECTING PEOPLE AND IDEAS

Match the item in column I with the description in column II.

	COLUMN I		COLUMN II
_____	1. Henry Bessemer and William Kelly	a.	Control of a market for certain goods or services by one or more companies.
_____	2. Thomas A. Edison	b.	Established the first oil well in Pennsylvania in 1859.
_____	3. William S. Burroughs	c.	People brought in by the employer to replace striking workers.
_____	4. Alexander Graham Bell	d.	Banker who combined steel companies to form the United States Steel Company in 1901.
_____	5. Edwin L. Drake	e.	Invented the typewriter in 1868.
_____	6. J. Frank Duryea	f.	Led the American Railway Union and was jailed during his participation in the Pullman strike.
_____	7. Christopher L. Sholes	g.	Scientific study and application of ideas and skills that are used to create machines and other innovative things.
_____	8. collective bargaining	h.	Developed the first incandescent electric bulb and inventor's laboratory.
_____	9. "robber barons"	i.	Built a one-cylinder gasoline engine in 1895.
_____	10. Samuel Gompers	j.	Invented the calculating or adding machine.
_____	11. Eugene V. Debs	k.	Developed a process for changing iron into steel.
_____	12. corporation	l.	Developed the first commercially useful telephone.
_____	13. monopoly	m.	A work stoppage by employees.
_____	14. anarchist	n.	Controlled the oil industry and did not care for competition.
_____	15. J. Pierpont Morgan	o.	Talented, ambitious, and often ruthless businessmen.
_____	16. Andrew Carnegie	p.	Workers who organized as a group to seek higher wages, better working conditions, and other benefits.
_____	17. John D. Rockefeller	q.	Discussions between union and employers to determine such things as wages, hours, and working conditions.
_____	18. labor unions	r.	Developed and controlled all aspects of the steel business.
_____	19. technology	s.	Founder of the American Federation of Labor.
_____	20. strike	t.	A business chartered or licensed by a state and owned by share-holding investors.
_____	21. strikebreakers	u.	Individual who favors doing away with all forms of government.

CREATING A BAR GRAPH

Study the following data and prepare a bar graph.

GAINFUL WORKERS, BY FARM-NONFARM OCCUPATIONS, 1850 TO 1910			
In thousands of persons 10 years old and over			
Year	Total Workers	Farm	Nonfarm
1850	7,697	4,902	2,795
1860	10,533	6,208	4,325
1870	12,925	6,850	6,075
1880	17,392	8,585	8,807
1890	23,318	9,938	13,380
1900	29,073	10,912	18,161
1910	37,371	11,592	25,779

Bar Graph:

Answer the following questions on a separate sheet of paper.

1. When did the number of nonfarm workers rise above the number of farm workers? Why do you think this happened?

2. When did the sharpest increase in the number of total workers occur? Why do you think this happened?

3. What other conclusions about nonfarm and farm workers can you draw by looking at your graph?

SUGGESTED TEACHING ACTIVITIES

1. Topics for further study:
   - a. Cyrus Field
   - b. Alexander G. Bell
   - c. Thomas A. Edison
   - d. Charles F. Brush
   - e. Henry Bessemer
   - f. William Kelly
   - g. Edwin L. Drake
   - h. Cornelius Vanderbilt
   - i. Andrew Carnegie
   - j. Leland Stanford
   - k. Jay Gould
   - l. John D. Rockefeller
   - m. Horatio Alger, Jr.
   - n. Henry George
   - o. Henry Clay Frick
   - p. Molly Maguires
   - q. Samuel Gompers
   - r. Eugene Debs
   - s. Pullman Strike
   - t. Haymarket Riot
   - u. Pinkerton Agency
   - v. child labor
   - w. working conditions

2. The growth of industry in this country brought forth men like John D. Rockefeller, head of the petroleum industry; Andrew Carnegie, steel producer; J. Pierpont Morgan, banker; Gustavus Swift, meat packer; and many others. It was believed by many that one should not interfere with competition in the marketplace. Government should leave businesses alone and the best or the fittest would naturally survive. If the business were productive, it would grow. The most competent or the best individual would become rich. It was believed that whatever survived in the corporate world was good. If you were poor, you must be either lazy or bad. There was nothing wrong with the economic system. Horatio Alger, Jr., wrote many popular books which used this rags-to-riches idea as their theme. He sold thousands of books which all contained a similar plot. It was the story of a poor individual who goes to the city, works hard, and becomes rich. People were inspired when they read his books and wanted to take advantage of the economic opportunities. Assign student volunteers to read one of the books written by Horatio Alger, Jr., and present a short report to the class. If more than one student volunteers, similarities among the books can be pointed out.

3. Organize a panel to discuss why individuals like Rockefeller, Carnegie, and Morgan were called "captains of industry" and "robber barons." Were these titles appropriate? Why or why not? Could philanthropists be "robber barons"? Why or why not? Would members of the Molly Maguires or other unions agree with you? Why or why not?

4. Assign students to draw cartoons showing the relationship between employees and employers and the relationship between "captains of industry" and government and the relationship between government and employees. Have students display their cartoons in the classroom and discuss the ideas which are depicted in them as to the problems and issues which arose from industrial development in this country.

5. Read selected chapters from George Larkin's *The Mill Girls* (New York: Tower Books, 1981) to the class. This is a story of a girl who left the farm to work in a textile mill in Lowell, Massachusetts. The mill girls worked 14 hours a day at the looms and were abused by their male overseers.

6. Assign students to find data regarding the number of immigrants who came to this country between 1860 and 1910 and prepare a graph. Then have them list all the ideas they learned from the graph about immigration during that period.

LIFE IN AMERICAN CITIES

More urban centers or cities were created or became more populated during the late 1800s. Some people who had lived on the farms were now leaving them to live in the cities. Cities offered more opportunities for employment and higher wages. Many modern conveniences were available to city dwellers such as specialty shops, restaurants, hot and cold water, streetcars, and department stores. Cities had libraries, museums, hospitals, churches, schools, and universities. Cities offered entertainment such as the theater, spectator sports, films, and vaudeville. At the same time, there were many hardships in city living which had not confronted Americans when most people lived in rural areas.

In spite of the problems in the cities, the urban population increased between 1860 and 1910. Black American families contributed to this growth. The violence and oppression of blacks in the South and the hopeless poverty led many of them to seek better opportunities in the northern cities. However, opportunities for them in the cities were limited. They tended to get positions in service occupations such as dishwashers, servants, and other menial jobs that paid very low salaries.

The largest source for population growth came from the arrival of new immigrants from many countries, particularly from southern and eastern Europe and China. The earlier immigrations came from Great Britain, Germany, and other northern European countries. Those people tended to settle in rural areas, except for the Irish who settled in cities on the east coast. Immigrants from China and southern and eastern Europe ate different foods, spoke different languages, and had different customs. These new immigrants had experienced poverty and sometimes religious and political oppression in their homelands. Coming to America was a promise for better economic opportunities to improve their lives. In most cases, these new immigrants had been farmers in their homelands and were now living in congested cities and in unsafe housing while they worked long hours in the factories, stockyards, and railroads. Because of their differences in language and lifestyle, they were often treated unfairly as they worked hard to learn English and adjust to the American way of life. To feel secure, they usually lived in communities, called *ghettos*, with others of similar ethnic and racial backgrounds.

Resentment against immigrants was obvious. Because of the large numbers of new immigrants, many native Americans reacted against the immigrants out of fear and prejudice. They accused the immigrants of being the cause of all the crime, problems, and corruption of city life. Many Americans felt that immigrant workers were taking jobs from other workers. People organized to control the number of immigrants gaining entry into the United States. They wanted to screen the immigrants by administering a literacy test and other standards designed to separate the desirable immigrants from the undesirable ones. In 1882 Congress voted to exclude the Chinese. It was now illegal for Chinese laborers to enter the United States. In the same year a general immigration act was passed which denied entry to certain "undesirables" and taxed every person admitted. In 1890 Congress expanded the list to limit more people and raised the tax fee. Powerful businesses opposed these restrictions since immigrants provided an unlimited cheap labor supply.

The expanding population in the cities produced poverty, crime, corrupt government, over-crowding, epidemics, and great fires. The problem of housing was a serious one. The wealthy were able to live in lovely, large homes away from industries. They were able to get to their offices in the city by streetcars and trolleys. For the poor, though, it was difficult to find a satisfactory place to live. Generally, makeshift houses and unsafe dwellings were available for them. Cities not only grew outward to accommodate the rapidly increasing population but also upward. Construction began on skyscrapers—some as tall as 10 stories.

Poverty and crime were to be found in the cities. Fires and diseases were even more devastating. Fires destroyed entire downtown sections and communities and caused many deaths. Cities developed fire departments and enacted laws regulating building construction for safety. Because of the increasing crime rate, police forces were organized by city governments. Crowded and poor living areas in the city caused high death rates from epidemics of diseases such as cholera, dysentery, and tuberculosis.

The political boss played an important role in the cities. The political boss tried to win as many votes for his party as he could. He befriended people living in the city, sometimes providing a bag of groceries for the needy, helping when someone was jailed for a petty crime, and finding jobs for possible voters.

Industrialization was changing the United States in many ways. People shopped for the new manufactured products in the department stores and mail-order houses; they took part as observers or participants in organized sports or leisure time activities; or they attended the theater, concerts, and vaudeville. Incomes were rising for almost everyone although at uneven rates. Most important was the growth of the middle class. Products in the stores were affordable. New merchandising techniques made many consumer goods available to everyone. Now, for the first time women could buy ready-made clothing. Changes occurred in the way Americans bought and prepared food. Mass production of tin cans created a large new industry devoted to packaging and selling canned food and condensed milk. Refrigerated railroad cars made it possible for perishable foods such as meats, vegetables, and dairy products to be transported over long distances without spoiling. National "chain stores" began to develop, and Sears Roebuck established a large market for its mail-order merchandise by making a catalog available to consumers in rural areas. Large department stores attracted shoppers.

Organized spectator sports became popular for men to enjoy. Baseball, football, and basketball players organized rules and leagues during this time. Golf and tennis, sports for the wealthy, had both men and women participants. Newspapers, books, and magazines were published for the masses of people. Theodore Dreiser, an American writer, encouraged authors to write about problems and issues in American society. Frank Norris published *The Octopus* in 1901. It is an interesting story of the struggle between oppressed wheat ranchers and powerful railroad interests in California. Another author, Upton Sinclair, in *The Jungle* exposed abuses in the American meat-packing industry. Mark Twain's *The Adventures of Huckleberry Finn* and Stephen Crane's *The Red Badge of Courage* were also widely read. Important changes were underway in American art. American artists such as Winslow Homer, John Singer Sargent, Edward Hopper, and George Bellows began to paint American scenes and developed an American style of painting. Cities built public art museums to display art works.

Industrialization depended upon specialized skills and scientific knowledge. An effective system of education was needed to produce people with these skills and knowledge. Universal free public education was expanded. The number of elementary and secondary schools increased, especially in the urban areas. Colleges and universities were founded. The number of women's colleges increased. Compulsory attendance laws were in effect in many states by 1900. John Dewey, an educator, believed that schools should help students acquire knowledge that would help them think. Charles E. Eliot, president of Harvard University, developed a curriculum which introduced the elective system and increased course offerings in the physical and social sciences, the fine arts, and modern languages.

THE ART GALLERY

Visit the local art museum or the library and find two paintings that depict American life during the late 1800s. Some of the artists from that period include James McNeill Whistler, John Sloan, George Bellows, John Singer Sargent, and Winslow Homer. Then complete the chart below:

	SELECTION ONE	SELECTION TWO
Title of painting	_____	_____
Artist's name	_____	_____
Where did you see this painting?	_____	_____
Tell something about the artist.	_____	_____
	_____	_____
	_____	_____
	_____	_____
	_____	_____
Describe the painting.	_____	_____
	_____	_____
	_____	_____
	_____	_____
	_____	_____
What does it tell you about American life in the late 1800s?	_____	_____
	_____	_____
	_____	_____
	_____	_____
	_____	_____

THE BIG CITIES

Study the following information about the 10 largest cities in the United States and then answer the questions.

LARGEST CITIES BY POPULATION, 1850–1900					
1850		1880		1900	
1. New York City	515,547	1. New York City	1,206,299	1. New York City	3,437,202
2. Baltimore	169,054	2. Philadelphia	847,170	2. Chicago	1,698,575
3. Boston	136,881	3. Chicago	503,185	3. Philadelphia	1,293,697
4. Philadelphia	121,376	4. Boston	362,839	4. St. Louis	575,238
5. New Orleans	116,375	5. St. Louis	350,518	5. Boston	560,892
6. Cincinnati	115,435	6. Baltimore	332,313	6. Baltimore	508,957
7. Brooklyn	96,838	7. Cincinnati	255,139	7. Cleveland	381,768
8. St. Louis	77,860	8. San Francisco	233,859	8. Buffalo, NY	352,387
9. Spring Garden, PA	58,894	9. New Orleans	216,090	9. San Francisco	342,782
10. Albany, NY	50,763	10. Washington, D.C.	177,624	10. Cincinnati	325,902

Note: Brooklyn was consolidated with New York in 1898. Spring Garden was annexed by Philadelphia in 1854.

1. Why do you think New York City has been the largest city in the United States for so many years?

_____

_____

2. Which city grew the fastest? Why do you think that city experienced such rapid growth?

_____

_____

3. Is the location of a city an important factor for its growth? Explain. What other factors are important in the growth of a city? Explain.

_____

_____

4. Check the United States Bureau of the Census or the most recent *Information Please Almanac* for the current list of the 10 largest cities. List them. As you compare the 1900 list to the current list, which cities still appear? Why do you think those cities are still the largest? Explain.

_____

_____

5. The population of the United States: 1850   23,191,876   1900   75,994,575
                                          1880   50,155,783   1990   248,709,873

List at least two other ideas you learned as you studied the lists of the largest cities and the population of the United States.

_____

_____

1. Topics for further study:

a. baseball league	f. skyscrapers	k. chain stores	p. universal education
b. basketball league	g. canned food	l. Edward Hopper	q. Upton Sinclair
c. football league	h. condensed milk	m. vaudeville	r. Mark Twain
d. tenements	i. John Philip Sousa	n. ghettos	s. Winslow Homer
e. mail-order houses	j. women's colleges	o. Scott Joplin	t. *Saturday Evening Post*

2. Duplicate the following chart on the chalkboard and ask students to study the data:

TOTAL IMMIGRATION, 1860–1900 (in thousands)			
Years	Number of Immigrants	Years	Number of Immigrants
1861 - 1865	802,000	1881 - 1885	2,976,000
1866 - 1870	1,513,000	1886 - 1890	2,271,000
1871 - 1875	1,727,000	1891 - 1895	2,124,000
1876 - 1880	1,086,000	1896 - 1900	1,564,000

Class discussion: In which years did the greatest number of immigrants arrive in the United States? In which years did the least number of immigrants arrive in the United States? What were the provisions of two immigration laws passed by Congress in 1882? How did these laws affect the number of immigrants who came to the United States?

3. Individual or group assignment: Assign students to make a study of the growth and development of a large city in their state. The study should emphasize the years after the Civil War until the turn of the century. Much of the information may be collected by visiting the city hall, interviewing senior citizens, or checking at the library. Why did the population of the city increase or decrease? Why did people want to live in that city? What attractions drew them to make their homes there? How was that city affected by industrialization? What kinds of factories developed in that city? Why? Which immigrant groups were most prominent in the city? Explain. Are there more people moving in or moving out of that city today? Why? A bulletin board can be designed to display all the information collected.

4. Assign a student volunteer to prepare an oral presentation on the Chicago fire of 1871 and the development of a professional fire department. Why were fires a threat? What changes were brought about by the citizens in the city regarding building laws?

5. Assign students to prepare a written or oral report on one of the immigrant groups, such as the Chinese, Italians, Germans, Greeks, Polish, Russians, Japanese, Finnish, or Irish. Why did they leave their homelands? Where did they settle in the United States after they arrived? How were they received? Why? What kind of work did they do? How did they adapt to the American customs and way of life? What contributions did they make to the American society?

6. Plan an educational trip to the local historical museum and/or the art museum to view artifacts and art works from the period after the Civil War until the turn of the century.

Suggestion for Supplementary Reading:
Smith, Bradley. *The U.S.A.: A History in Art.* Garden City, NY: A Gemini Smith Inc., Book— Doubleday & Company, Inc., 1975.

HARD TIMES AND POLITICS IN AMERICA

During the late 1800s, the United States faced many problems. However, the leadership in government had few ideas about what to do about them. Neither political party took a stand on monopolies, the conflict between labor and management, farm problems, or the economic depressions experienced by the nation. Political parties were mainly interested in winning elections. This allowed the party bosses to control the appointment of party members to government jobs. Sometimes the president felt powerless as the bosses awarded jobs to faithful party members. One group within the Republican party wanted civil service reform, but another group opposed any reform in how government jobs were to be awarded.

When President Garfield died from a bullet shot by a disgruntled government job seeker, Chester A. Arthur became president of the United States. President Arthur supported a high protective tariff. He believed that federal troops should remain in the South. He also required officeholders to make party contributions. The Pendleton Act, signed by President Arthur in 1883, reestablished the Civil Service Commission and extended the merit system. This Act also made it illegal to demand that federal employees contribute to a party's campaign or to fire a competent employee for political reasons.

The next presidential election held in 1884 was won by the Republican candidate, Grover Cleveland. He wanted to make the federal government more efficient. He did not take positions on political issues, and he believed that government should not interfere with expanding businesses. He did, though, introduce a bill which reduced tariffs, but the bill did not pass. In the election of 1888, Benjamin Harrison, Republican, became president. He was faced with the issue of controlling the power of trusts that discouraged competition in the marketplace. The Sherman Antitrust Act was passed in 1890. This was the first federal law to regulate the practices of businesses. Also in 1890, Congress passed the highest protective tariffs yet, the McKinley Tariff Act.

People were angry because they believed that the cost of living was too high. They believed that high protective tariffs were to blame because they kept prices high. The cost of their food, housing, clothing, and other necessities was more than they could comfortably afford. During his administration, President Cleveland did enact a law that made moderate reductions in the general tariff rate but offered special protection to certain large trusts. Congress, in 1887, passed the Interstate Commerce Act that prohibited discrimination in rates between long and short hauls and other unpopular railroad practices. The law also required railroads to publish their rate schedules and file them with the government. All fees for interstate rail transportation were to be "reasonable and just." Congress, though, failed to give the Interstate Commerce Commission the authority to enforce the act.

The lives of the American farmers were changing. Farmers no longer consisted of independent families, living on small farms. New farm machinery made it possible to own bigger farms and produce more crops. Sometimes the farmers grew too much. When this happened, they had to sell their produce at lower prices. They had to mortgage their farms to get the money to buy farm machinery and other necessities if the weather conditions reduced or destroyed their crops and livestock. They felt that the railroad charged high rates to ship their products to market. They opposed high tariffs because they believed high tariffs drove prices too high for the goods people wanted. They felt the government was helping the big companies avoid competition with foreign products at their expense. There were many economic depressions, when business did poorly and people were out of work. The farmers were directly affected during these difficult times.

Shortly after the Civil War the farmers organized the Grange. This organization tried to bring the farmers together to learn new scientific farming techniques. Also, the Grange hoped to create a feeling of community among the members. Cooperative political action was urged to limit the power of the monopoly of railroads and warehouses. The Grange set up cooperative stores, creameries, elevators, warehouses, insurance companies, and factories that produced machines and other items. The Grange was not very successful because of its inexperience and the opposition of merchants whose businesses it was challenging. State legislators who were supportive of the program were elected. The Grange wanted the railroads under government control. The organization eventually weakened and lost membership.

Farmers' alliances began to form and grow rapidly in the 1880s. Their goals were quite similar to those of the Grange but they formed a more powerful organization. They also organized cooperatives and influenced the government to control prices and monopolies. Women had full voting rights in most alliances. Many held offices and served as lecturers. The alliances formed the Populist party. Populism attracted many small farmers who needed a sense of belonging to a community. Populist leaders were members of the rural middle class: professional people, editors and lawyers, or long-time politicians. Few were farmers.

The Populists supported a program of reform to meet the needs of individuals and communities. They believed that society had an obligation to protect the well-being of its individual citizens. Populists challenged the way the American economy was developing and forming. They wanted a just and stable society. They proposed many ideas. They felt that the government should provide loans to farmers at low rates of interest. They wanted an end of absentee ownership of land. They advocated the direct election of United States senators. They supported government ownership of railroads, telephones, and telegraphs. They advocated a graduated income tax. When

GRANGE MEETING

Grover Cleveland, in the presidential election of 1892, defeated their candidate, James B. Weaver, for the presidency, the party lost most of its membership. Many Populist ideas, though, were later adopted by the government.

A severe economic depression, a time of slow business activity and unemployment, created widespread economic and political unrest. In 1894 Jacob S. Coxey, a member of the Populist party, organized about 500 unemployed workers to march to Washington on foot from Ohio. When they reached the Capitol, they were met by armed policemen. Coxey was arrested and convicted of walking on the grass. Congress took no action on the workers' demands. There were other protests such as the Homestead and Pullman strikes.

President Cleveland believed that public fear about the value of the dollar was the primary cause of the depression. The basic issue was what would form the basis of the dollar—that is, what would lie behind it and give it value. Money, in the nineteenth century, was assumed to be worthless if there were not gold or silver behind it. Farmers wanted more money in the market as a means of raising the prices of farm products and easing payment of their debts. Money became the most important issue in the presidential election of 1896. The Democrats nominated the "silver-tongued" William Jennings Bryan for president. He believed that "free silver" would create more money and bring an end to economic depressions. He was defeated by his Republican opponent, William McKinley of Ohio. In 1898, during President McKinley's administration, prosperity began to return to America.

When President McKinley was inaugurated a second time in 1901, the country was in a state of prosperity. The government focused attention on the need for higher tariff rates. The Dingley tariff was passed, raising the duties to an average of 57 percent—the highest in history. Business and government were working together. The Gold Standard Act of 1900 committed the United States to the gold standard. This meant that gold would be used as a basis for determining the value of money. Therefore, a person could demand an exchange of paper money for gold. Each dollar was backed by an equal amount of gold. The McKinley presidency brought about tariff increases, the gold standard, and prosperity.

Name_____

CONNECTING WORDS AND DEFINITIONS

Match the items in column I with their descriptions in column II.

COLUMN I	COLUMN II
_____ 1. anti-trust	a. Period of slow business activity, causing an increase in unemployment and low prices.
_____ 2. tariff	b. Monopoly formed by uniting several companies into one system under a board of trustees.
_____ 3. civil service	c. To be opposed to trusts, monopolies, or any other type of agreement that fixes prices to control trade.
_____ 4. depression	d. Taxes placed on imported goods by the government.
_____ 5. trust	e. Practice of giving government jobs to party supporters after victory on election day.
_____ 6. merit system	f. Business owned and operated by its workers.
_____ 7. cooperative	g. System of employment determined by merit or competitive examinations.
_____ 8. gold standard	h. The exclusive control by a company to determine the price, quality, and quantity of a particular product or service.
_____ 9. mortgage	i. Taxes on imports high enough to protect American industry against foreign competition.
_____ 10. spoils system	j. Use of gold as the basis for money; the ability to exchange paper money for the legal amount of gold on demand.
_____ 11. monopoly	k. To use property as security for a loan from a lender.
_____ 12. prosperity	l. Interaction between two or more states in the United States.
_____ 13. cost of living	m. Tax system which allows people to pay according to their income. If their income is higher, they pay higher taxes.
_____ 14. interstate	n. Time when people are employed and businesses are successful and growing.
_____ 15. graduated income tax	o. The average cost of the necessities of life such as food, shelter, clothing, and health expenses.
_____ 16. protective tariff	p. Government jobs for which appointments are made on merit (by examinations) rather than on political favor.

PRESIDENTIAL ELECTIONS

Study the following chart:

Year	Candidates	Parties	Popular Vote	Percentage of Popular Vote	Electoral Vote	Percentage of Voter Participation
1876	**Rutherford B. Hayes**	Republican	4,036,298	48.0%	185	81.8%
	Samuel J. Tilden	Democratic	4,300,590	51.0%	184	
1880	**James A. Garfield**	Republican	4,454,416	48.5%	214	79.4%
	Winfield S. Hancock	Democratic	4,444,952	48.1%	155	
1884	**Grover Cleveland**	Democratic	4,874,986	48.5%	219	77.5%
	James G. Blaine	Republican	4,851,981	48.2%	182	
1888	**Benjamin Harrison**	Republican	5,439,853	47.9%	233	79.3%
	Grover Cleveland	Democratic	5,540,309	48.6%	168	
1892	**Grover Cleveland**	Democratic	5,556,918	46.1%	277	74.7%
	Benjamin Harrison	Republican	5,176,108	43.0%	145	
	James B. Weaver	People's	1,041,028	8.5%	22	
1896	**William McKinley**	Republican	7,104,799	51.1%	271	79.3%
	William J. Bryan	Democratic-People's	6,502,925	47.7%	176	
1900	**William McKinley**	Republican	7,207,923	51.7%	292	73.2%
	William J. Bryan	Democratic-Populist	6,358,133	45.5%	155	

Answer the following questions:

1. Which political party was in power during most of the presidential administrations between 1876 and 1900?

_____

2. During which election was the percentage of voter participation the highest?

_____

3. What was most interesting about the elections of 1876 and 1888?

_____

_____

4. What kind of candidate was William J. Bryan? Explain.

_____

_____

5. Why do you think the number of total electoral votes increased between President Hayes' election in 1876 and President McKinley's election in 1900?

_____

_____

SUGGESTED TEACHING ACTIVITIES

1. Topics for further study:
   a. civil service reform
   b. President James A. Garfield
   c. Charles J. Guiteau
   d. President Chester A. Arthur
   e. President Benjamin Harrison
   f. William Jennings Bryan
   g. President William McKinley
   h. President Grover Cleveland
   i. Populist Party
   j. Jacob S. Coxey
   k. Grange
   l. Mary Ellen Lease

2. Class Discussion: Chester A. Arthur became president of the United States when President James A. Garfield died after being shot by an assassin. He was a skilled politician who enjoyed being a political boss by rewarding party members with government jobs after a victorious election. When he became president, though, his friends felt he had become a different or a "new" Chester A. Arthur. Why did they say this? What was one of the major achievements during his administration? Is it possible that the "office of United States presidency" can make a person reexamine his values and lift him above party politics? Review the Pendleton Civil Service Act passed in 1883. What were the provisions of the Act? Why was it passed? What are the differences between the spoils system and the merit system? Do you think it is fair to have to take a competitive examination for a government position? Explain.

3. Have students draw cartoons illustrating the conflict between the farmers and the railroad companies and/or the conflict between farmers and high protective tariffs. Display the cartoons in the classroom and discuss the issues illustrated.

4. Assign students to pretend that they are newspaper reporters attending the Democratic convention in 1896 and have just heard William Jennings Bryan deliver a speech. Either write an article for the newspaper telling who, where, when, what, and why or write an editorial for your newspaper, stating your position about his nomination for presidency.

5. As a class prepare a list of the reforms that were favored by the Populists. Which three did they consider to be the most important and why? Did the Populists have any political strength? Explain. Were any of their reforms enacted into law? Which ones? A helpful resource: Johnson, Donald Bruce, and Kirk H. Porter, (compilers). *National Party Platforms: 1840–1972*. Urbana, IL: University of Illinois Press, 1973.

6. Assign students to work in groups to draw two murals. One should illustrate the changes being experienced in farm life during the late 1800s. The other should illustrate the grievances and/or problems faced by the farmers during the same period.

7. With the participation of the entire class, prepare a time line to display in the classroom—noting the date and possibly an illustration for at least 10 significant events which occurred during this time period. Add other events to this time line as you study the history of the United States.

8. Prepare a display entitled "Money in the United States." In 1785 the Congress adopted the dollar as the U. S. unit of money. The first United States money was made in 1792. Show the important features of United States paper money, types of money, the designing of money, how to tell counterfeit money, etc. Some books which may be helpful follow:
   Cooke, David C. *How Money Is Made*. Revised Edition. New York: Dodd, Mead & Company, 1972.
   Cribb, Joe. *Eyewitness Books: Money*. New York: Alfred A. Knopf, 1990.
   Russell, Solveig Paulson. *From Barter to Gold: The Story of Money*. Chicago: Rand McNally & Company, 1961.

BECOMING A WORLD POWER

When George Washington assumed the presidency of the United States, he warned the country to avoid involvement in the disputes and politics of foreign nations. His warning was heeded, but with industrialization the attitude toward other nations was changing. Alfred Thayer Mahan, naval admiral and historian, maintained that Americans had to become involved with the world. The American economy needed new markets for its growing surpluses of manufactured goods and farm products. According to Admiral Mahan the nations with sea power were the great nations. Therefore, the United States had to develop its sea power. Overseas expansion would bring economic prosperity. There were those, too, who did not agree with American expansion.

Secretary of State James G. Blaine believed that the United States was destined to be a world power. Because he thought that Latin America would serve as an excellent market for American businesses, he aided in organizing the Pan-American Union in 1881. Great Britain and Venezuela, in 1895, were involved in a serious boundary dispute between British Guiana and Venezuela. Americans were sympathetic to Venezuela. The United States sent a note to Great Britain proposing a plan to solve the dispute. Great Britain was reluctant to agree to any plan. Faced with threats from Germany and Japan, Great Britain finally agreed to discuss and settle the boundary dispute.

The islands of Hawaii in the mid-Pacific attracted many Americans. Missionaries, planters, and business people came and invested in the coffee and sugar plantations. They were able to gain control of the major industries and political power. The United States Navy considered Pearl Harbor, on the island of Oahu, an excellent base for its ships and an important coaling station for commercial ships. In 1887 the Americans forced a new constitution on the Hawaiians. The Queen of Hawaii, Liliuokalani, abolished the constitution. The American settlers then organized a revolution and overthrew her. A government was set up by the Americans who negotiated for a treaty, in 1893, for Hawaii's annexation to the United States.

The treaty of annexation was sent by President Harrison to the Senate for ratification. The United States was to assume the Hawaiian debt of $2,000,000 and pay the queen a pension of $20,000 a year. Before the treaty was ratified, Congress recessed. Finally, in 1898, Hawaii was annexed by Congress.

The Samoan islands, south of Hawaii, served as a station for American commercial ships. As trade increased with Asia, business people and the navy thought it important that Americans have the use of the harbor, Pago Pago, on the island of Tutuila. In 1878 a treaty was approved by the Senate, providing for an American naval station at Pago Pago and committing the United States to use its power to adjust Samoa's conflicts with foreign nations. In 1899 the United States and Germany divided the islands between themselves. Great Britain was given territories elsewhere in the Pacific. Germany obtained the two largest islands, but the United States kept the harbor at Pago Pago.

Cuba, an island in the Caribbean, had belonged to Spain since its discovery by Columbus. Dishonest officials and heavy taxation led the Cubans to rebel against the Spaniards. The newspapers wrote sensational stories about the happenings in Cuba. They printed pictures showing the cruel treatment inflicted by the Spaniards and made people in the United States excited about the events in Cuba. The United States expressed sympathy and urged Cubans to fight for independence. The United States battleship *Maine*, while in Havana harbor, sank after a terrific explosion. The episode about the *Maine* was greatly exaggerated by the newspapers as they made a number of accusations against the Spanish government. Even today, the cause of the explosion is not known. "Remember the *Maine!*" became the words urging war against Spain. Congress, in 1898, recognized Cuba's independence and demanded that Spain leave Cuba. Spain, of course, refused and declared war on the United States.

War was declared in April and it was over in August. John Hay, Secretary of State, described the Spanish-American war as a "a splendid little war." Theodore Roosevelt, Assistant Secretary of the Navy, resigned his position to fight with the Rough Riders in Cuba. The Rough Riders were a cavalry regiment of cowboys, college students, bear hunters, gamblers, and others. The Cuban rebels had already weakened the Spanish soldiers before the American troops entered into the war. The American forces were poorly organized and poorly prepared to fight.

When war was declared, Theodore Roosevelt ordered Commodore George Dewey to attack the Philippine Islands in the Pacific. This was the first victory of the Spanish-American War as Commodore Dewey took Manila, the capital of the Philippine Islands. In Cuba, the Rough Riders attacked San Juan Hill and entrenched themselves on the hills to the east of Santiago. The next day, the American fleet destroyed the Spanish ships and the commander of the Spaniards surrendered the city of Santiago to the Americans. Spain, weak and incompetent, was defeated.

The Spanish government asked for peace and the war ended in August. Spain recognized the independence of Cuba and gave Puerto Rico to the United States. Spain also turned over to the Americans the Pacific island of Guam. President McKinley was not certain what to do about the Philippines. Finally, he decided to annex the islands to the United States. The Americans offered to pay $20,000,000 for the Philippines and the treaty was signed. In six weeks the United States had an overseas empire which industrialized nations, such as Great Britain, Germany, and others, had begun many years earlier.

The conflict with the Philippines is something that Americans would like to forget. It lasted from 1899 to 1902 and it was a cruel war. The Filipinos had rebelled against the Spaniards even before 1898. They believed that Admiral George Dewey and his forces would give them independence. When General Emilio Aguinaldo, leader of the Filipino rebels, learned that the United States had purchased the Philippines from the Spanish as a part of the peace treaty with Spain, the Filipinos rebelled against the Americans. Finally, General Aguinaldo was captured. He signed a document urging his followers to stop fighting and declared his allegiance to the United States. In 1906 Americans took possession of the Philippines. William Howard Taft established a civilian government which built schools, roads, and hospitals. In 1946 the islands gained their independence from the United States.

When the United States acquired the Philippines, Americans became interested in increasing trade in the Far East. John Hay, Secretary of State, asked a number of nations to respect the rights of all countries and to keep an "open door" for trading with China. The responses were vague but Secretary Hay announced that the major powers had approved. The Boxers, Chinese men who resented foreign influence in their country, began a rebellion to destroy the power of Americans and Europeans in China. The foreigners hid in the British Embassy until a relief army captured the city of Peking and rescued them. The foreigners were freed and the Chinese paid for the damages resulting from the rebellion. Secretary Hay sent a new note to the European nations declaring that America supported an "open door policy" regarding trade in China, and everyone agreed to participate.

The war with Spain led the United States to reform the military system by making it better organized and more efficient. The size of the regular army was increased. It established federal supervision of the National Guard. Officer training schools were founded. In 1903 a general staff headed by a chief of staff was established. The chief of staff acted as military adviser to the Secretary of War. With these reforms, the United States entered the twentieth century as a major world power.

MAP STUDY

TERRITORIAL EXPANSION OF THE UNITED STATES			
Territory	Date Acquired	Square Miles	How Acquired
Original states and territories	1783	888,685	Treaty with Great Britain
Louisiana Purchase	1803	827,192	Purchase from France
Florida	1819	72,003	Treaty with Spain
Texas	1845	390,143	Annexation of independent nation
Oregon	1846	285,580	Treaty with Great Britain
Mexican Cession	1848	529,017	Conquest from Mexico
Gadsden Purchase	1853	29,640	Purchase from Mexico
Alaska	1867	589,757	Purchase from Russia
Hawaii	1898	6,450	Annexation of independent nation
The Philippines	1899	115,600	Conquest from Spain (granted independence in 1946)
Puerto Rico	1899	3,435	Conquest from Spain
Guam	1899	212	Conquest from Spain
American Samoa	1900	76	Treaty with Germany and Great Britain

On the outline map of the world identify the location of the listed territories.

Name_____

IF YOU HAD BEEN . . .

Write a short paragraph explaining your position on each of the three following situations. Give evidence to support your action.

1. If you had been a student at Yale University in 1898, would you have volunteered to serve in the first United States volunteer cavalry regiment (the Rough Riders) to fight in Cuba? Why or why not?

_____

_____

_____

_____

_____

_____

_____

2. If you had been a United States senator in 1898, would you have voted to annex the Philippines to the United States? Why or why not?

_____

_____

_____

_____

_____

_____

_____

3. If you had been a United States senator in 1898, would you have voted to annex Hawaii to the United States? Why or why not?

_____

_____

_____

_____

_____

_____

_____

SUGGESTED TEACHING ACTIVITIES

1. Topics for further study:
   a. Alfred Thayer Mahan
   b. James G. Blaine
   c. Pan-American Union
   d. Hawaii
   e. Queen Liliuokalani
   f. Pearl Harbor
   g. Pago Pago
   h. Cuba
   i. Puerto Rico
   j. Boxer Rebellion
   k. *Maine* incident
   l. yellow journalism
   m. Philippines
   n. Rough Riders
   o. Theodore Roosevelt
   p. open door policy
   q. San Juan Hill
   r. Manila

2. Ask the class to assume that they are advisers to President McKinley. On the chalkboard, prepare a list of the advantages and disadvantages of annexing the Philippines to the United States. Discuss the information presented by class members.

3. Assign individual students or groups of students to study one of the territories the United States acquired: Alaska, Hawaii, the Philippines, Puerto Rico, Guam, or American Samoa. Write a report providing the following information:
   a. Where is it located? How near is it to the United States?
   b. How did it become a possession of the United States?
   c. Describe the territory geographically. Identify large cities and important geographical features.
   d. What kind of people live in that territory? How do they make a living? How do they govern themselves?
   e. What are its major imports and exports?
   f. What is its political status today?

4. Read the book, *Bully for You, Teddy Roosevelt!* written by Jean Fritz (New York: G. P. Putnam's Sons, 1991) orally to the class. Jean Fritz is an excellent author whose style of writing is especially appealing to young people. The book presents the story of Theodore Roosevelt from boyhood through his presidency in the United States.

5. Student volunteers may wish to prepare a large map of the world to display in the classroom showing all of the possessions acquired by the United States between 1803 and 1900. Important geographical features should be pointed out.

6. Have students prepare a bar graph showing the amount of square miles acquired for each territory by the United States between 1803 and 1900. Which territory was the largest in size? The smallest in size? Which territory was most important to the United States? The least important to the United States? Explain.

7. Student volunteers may wish to make a special study of the ships used by the United States in the Spanish-American War. Illustrations of the ships could be displayed on the bulletin board in the classroom and compared to the ships in the United States Navy today.

Suggestions for Supplementary Reading:

Kent, Zachary. *The Story of the Rough Riders*. Cornerstones of Freedom. Chicago: Childrens Press, 1991.

---. *The Sinking of the Battleship* Maine. Cornerstones of Freedom. Chicago: Childrens Press, 1988.

Tabrah, Ruth. *Hawaii: A Bicentennial History*. New York: W. W. Norton & Company, Inc., 1980.

Tope, Lily Rose R. *Philippines: Cultures of the World*. New York: Marshall Cavendish Corporation, 1991.

THE PROGRESSIVE MOVEMENT

Industrialization brought about many changes. The American way of life was changing; there were more conveniences. The ideas and things people thought were important and valuable were changing. There were other problems, such as poverty, injustice, discrimination, and crime. Many people, particularly those known as the *progressives* or reformers, believed that new ways had to be discovered to bring about greater justice, equality, and security in the American society. They also believed in the idea of progress and improvement to guarantee a better life for Americans. They acknowledged that government should have a role in the process of bringing about reforms. Only government could successfully oppose those who were corrupting the country. Services and regulations could be provided by the government that would bring about benefits for everyone.

The progressives wanted to limit the power of monopolies. Power and authority, they felt, should be divided among the people more equitably. Most reformers believed that the individual had responsibilities to society and society had responsibilities to the individual. Regulations and just laws were necessary to bring about order and stability to the American society.

Theodore Roosevelt accused journalists of "raking up muck" when they wrote newspaper and magazine articles or books that exposed dishonesty, injustices, and corruption in society. A "muck" was a rake for cleaning dirt from the floor. Ida Tarbell, a muckraker, wrote about her study of the Standard Oil Company. She explained how John D. Rockefeller and his partners had built the oil industry monopoly. Lincoln Steffens, another influential muckraker, wrote a series of articles about crime and corruption in city government. He strongly believed that people should take a greater interest in public life. *The Jungle*, a novel written by Upton Sinclair, told how diseased and unhealthy animals were slaughtered in the stockyards. Soon after that book was published in 1906, the Pure Food and Drug Act and Meat Inspection Act were passed. The muckrakers explored child labor, immigrant ghettos, and many other problems. Their readers were developing a sense of responsibility and a concern for personal injustice.

The Salvation Army, organized in the United States in 1879, offered both aid and spiritual help to the poor. The Salvation Army established missions in many cities and provided food, clothing, and shelter for the needy and unemployed. Jane Addams established the first settlement house, Hull House, in Chicago. Addams, a college graduate, helped immigrant families adapt to the language and customs of their new country. Settlement houses offered educational services, staged community events, and provided many other activities to improve the lives of the people in the urban neighborhoods. Hull House became a model for the establishment of other settlement houses in many other American cities. Many college women found the work in the settlement houses to be satisfying and rewarding.

During the early 1900s, a new middle class emerged, based on educational qualifications and individual accomplishment. Standards were applied to the professions, restricting entry unless certain requirements were met. American women found themselves excluded from most of the professions, such as medicine and law. Managing settlement houses, teaching, nursing, and library work were traditional and acceptable professions for women. Many women joined the Temperance Movement, an organization to outlaw alcoholic beverages. Some women joined the new women's clubs and became involved in public matters and reform. At first, they were involved in non-controversial projects, such as planting trees; supporting schools, libraries, and settlement houses; and building hospitals and parks. As the progressive movement grew stronger, they supported more controversial projects such as child labor laws, women's suffrage, worker's compensation laws, and pure food and drug legislation.

Reformers knew they needed the cooperation of government to enact laws to protect women and child laborers and to improve conditions in the ghettos. Government could provide regulations and control to impose order and justice in society. Government, itself, needed to be reformed. Most states had adopted the secret ballot. Party rule could be broken by increasing the power of the people through the use of the referendum and the initiative. This made it possible for the reformers to go directly to the people in general elections. Laws were passed restricting lobbying by business interests in state legislatures.

People began to take a renewed interest in government. They challenged the powerful city bosses, their political organizations, and special-interest groups. Many cities throughout the United States removed city government from politics by reorganizing the cities into a commission type of government or the city-manager system. Elected mayors, such as Thomas L. Johnson of Cleveland, introduced many reforms, such as appointing competent officials and eliminating unfair business privileges. "Fighting" Bob La Follette, governor of Wisconsin, supported many reforms such as the graduated income tax on inherited fortunes, regulation of the workplace, providing compensation for workers injured on the job, and taxation of railroad companies according to the value of their properties, not their earnings.

The political parties changed to keep their influence and power. New York's Tammany Hall, the nation's oldest city machine, maintained power while assuming responsibility of some of the concerns of social reformers. Charles Francis Murphy, one of the leaders in Tammany Hall, used its political power to improve working conditions, protect child laborers, and eliminate the worst abuses in industry. In 1911 the Triangle Shirtwaist Company was swept by a fire which killed 146 workers, almost all of them women. They had been trapped inside the building because the management had locked the emergency exits to prevent

people from taking breaks from their work. It was the worst tragedy in the city's history. Tammany Hall pressured for new laws that imposed strict building codes on factory owners and established regular inspections and enforcement of the laws.

Campaigns to eliminate the use of alcoholic beverages from national life were waged by many groups. Frances Willard, president of the Women's Christian Temperance Union (WCTU), urged women to take an active role in eliminating the use of intoxicating beverages. The Anti-Saloon League of America, formed in 1895, advocated the elimination of alcohol as a necessary task in restoring order to society. Finally, Congress approved the Eighteenth Amendment. The Amendment to our federal constitution that took effect in January 1920 prohibited the "manufacture, sale, or transportation of intoxicating liquors."

Demands were made to restrict immigration at this time. Some Americans felt the continued arrival of foreigners was creating urban problems, overcrowding, unemployment, and social unrest. Demands were also being made for women's suffrage. Some supporters believed that giving women the right to vote would strengthen the reform movement. To many men, and even to many women, the idea of women having the right to vote seemed threatening. By 1919 women had been granted the right to vote in 39 states in at least some elections. In 1920 the suffragists won approval of the Nineteenth Amendment which guaranteed political rights to women throughout the United States.

Reform in America was progressing slowly. Yet, the change in the role of government was noticeable. Before the 1900s local, state, or federal governments did very little to help people or to regulate any aspect of everyday life or the economy. The progressive movement made Americans reconsider the role and responsibility of government. Laws were passed to improve working conditions. Women were finally given the right to vote. The reform movement, however, did not solve all problems.

MAKING CONNECTIONS

Explain the ways in which the item in Column I is connected to the corresponding item in Column II.

COLUMN I		COLUMN II
1. *The Jungle*	_____	Pure Food and Drug Act
2. Jane Addams	_____	Hull House
3. Salvation Army	_____	urban poor
4. Thomas L. Johnson	_____	Cleveland
5. Suffragists	_____	Nineteenth Amendment
6. Muckrakers	_____	Lincoln Steffens
7. Tammany Hall	_____	Triangle Shirtwaist Fire
8. Robert La Follette	_____	Wisconsin

Name_____

WHAT DOES IT MEAN?

Connect the definitions in Column II with the terms they define in Column I.

COLUMN I

_____1. muckrakers

_____2. referendum

_____3. progressive movement

_____4. negotiation

_____5. arbitration

_____6. settlement house

_____7. suffrage

_____8. temperance movement

_____9. lobbying

_____10. initiative

_____11. commission city government

COLUMN II

a. The elected commissioners serve collectively as the city council and separately as heads of the city's various departments.

b. The activities of an agent for a pressure group, usually to influence the passage or defeat of certain legislation.

c. A process by which a certain percentage of the voters can put a proposed law or constitutional amendment on the ballot for popular approval or rejection in a state election.

d. An urban neighborhood center providing social services, such as cooperative housing for young working women, a nursery, educational programs, and nursing for immigrants and the poor.

e. Journalists who investigated and exposed corruption and dishonest practices in society through their articles and books.

f. A process in which a proposed new law or change in an existing law passed by a state legislature is submitted or referred to the voters for final approval or rejection.

g. A campaign against the consumption or use of alcoholic beverages.

h. A process by which the parties involved in a dispute discuss their differences with an impartial individual or group and then arrive at an acceptable decision.

i. Particular groups demanding progress and reform in society and government, usually members of the middle class.

j. A process involving discussion and bargaining to arrive at an acceptable agreement.

k. The right to vote.

SUGGESTED TEACHING ACTIVITIES

1. Topics for further study:
   a. Theodore Roosevelt
   b. Lincoln Steffens
   c. Ida Tarbell
   d. Jane Addams
   e. Thomas L. Johnson
   f. Salvation Army
   g. settlement houses
   h. Charles Francis Murphy
   i. Triangle Shirtwaist factory fire
   j. Robert M. La Follette
   k. Anti-Saloon League of America
   l. Women's Christian Temperance Union
   m. women's suffrage

2. The discussions and campaigns for women's right to vote began in 1848. This occurred at the first women's rights convention at Seneca Falls, New York. The founders of the Women's Rights Movement were the first woman candidate for president, Victoria Woodhull, Lucretia Mott, Elizabeth Cady Stanton, Lucy Stone, and Susan B. Anthony. At that meeting, which was attended by Elizabeth Cady Stanton, Lucretia Mott, and many others, a women's declaration of independence was written. In 1920 the Nineteenth Amendment to the Constitution was approved. "The right of citizens of the United States to vote shall not be denied or abridged by the United States or by any State on account of sex." Class Discussion: Why do you think it took so long to get this right passed? What were some of the views about women, marriage, and being a housewife and mother believed in the late 1800s and early 1900s? How have attitudes and views about women and their roles in society changed today? Explain.

3. Assign students to imagine they are young adults in the year 1900 and to select one reform movement, such as women's right to vote, Temperance Movement, limiting power of monopolies, curbing powers of party bosses, or removing corrupt city governments. Tell why you selected that reform movement and what you want to do and hope to accomplish by joining the reform group in a short composition. Students can share these papers with their classmates in an informal class discussion.

4. Assign students to prepare one-page fliers inviting people to join the Women's Christian Temperance Union or the Anti-Saloon League of America. The fliers should be attractive, include the name and purpose of the organization, and the place and time of meeting. Display the fliers in the classroom.

5. Arrange an educational field trip to the local Salvation Army and/or invite a representative from the Salvation Army to the classroom to discuss the services it provides for the community and how one can volunteer to help.

6. Student volunteers may prepare a list of all the organizations within their community that assist people who are in need. Perhaps a representative from one of those organizations may be invited to speak to the class about his or her work.

7. As a class, prepare a list of reforms students would like to see in their community and/or in their school that would lead toward improvement for everyone. Perhaps one of the reforms can be selected and students can become involved in a community or school project.

8. Student volunteers may prepare a list (bibliography) of fiction and nonfiction books about progressive leaders and reforms to be found in the school media center or library and share it with their classmates.

Highlights in American History

ENTERING THE TWENTIETH CENTURY

When President McKinley died in September 1901, killed by an assassin, Theodore Roosevelt, a popular hero, became president of the United States. Before becoming vice president under President McKinley, he had been a rancher, a Rough Rider in the Spanish-American War, and governor of New York. He was a tremendously energetic and enthusiastic young man of 42 years of age when he became the youngest president of the United States. He had many ideas and interests, and he strongly believed that our system of government should benefit all the people, not certain groups only.

President Roosevelt believed in the importance of efficient government. As president, he would be the "center" of the action, a strong leader, dealing with Congress and the people. He believed in the American economic system; he also believed that everyone should have a "square deal." For instance, according to President Roosevelt, the government should investigate the activities of corporations and publicize the findings in newspapers. If the corporations were involved in dishonest and unfair practices, public opinion would eliminate most of these corporate abuses.

The progressives generally worked at the local and state governmental levels to bring about changes. Especially, though, in situations dealing with the economy, it appeared to some reformers that the federal government needed to act. President Roosevelt, soon after his inauguration, made it clear that he planned to introduce, direct, and hinder, if necessary, Congressional legislation on behalf of the interests and needs of the American people. In his first message to Congress, he listed a number of reforms such as federal regulation of corporations, development of forest reserves, strengthening of the navy, and the building of a system of federal reservoirs and canals in the West.

He did not challenge the monopolies created by the corporations. He believed that corporations were necessary in modern industry. Many corporations had received valuable government assistance and favors in establishing their companies. However, he soon realized that corporations which formed monopolies and charged outrageous prices for necessities such as coal, oil, sugar, and other products should be regulated by the government. President Roosevelt felt they should not be making huge profits at the expense of the public welfare. He believed government should serve as a mediator between the interests of the people and the corporations.

President Roosevelt was the first president to listen to the concerns of the workers. When it appeared that a severe strike called by the United Mine Workers in the anthracite mines in Pennsylvania would cause suffering during the winter of 1902, the president called representatives of the strikers and the owners of the mines to a meeting at the White House to settle the dispute. The miners received a 10 percent wage increase (the first in 20 years) although they had asked for 20 percent and a nine-hour work day. The public was relieved that the strike ended. The Constitution does not state specifically that a president has the right to intervene in a dispute between management and employees. But, President Roosevelt did, giving the workers a "square deal," and his popularity increased.

President Roosevelt was a naturalist, sportsman, and a conservationist. He was concerned about the unregulated misuse of America's natural resources. He appointed a conservationist, Gifford Pinchot, to head the United States Forest Service. They both believed in the careful management of public lands and protection of the environment for future generations. During his presidency, he brought the area of government reserved forest and mineral lands up to more than 150 million acres. The Reclamation Act, passed in 1902, made it possible to fund the irrigation of lands which were sold to the settlers at moderate prices. President Roosevelt's greatest service to this nation was in the conservation of the environment.

The Dominican Republic owed money to certain European nations whose leaders wanted to collect it by force. President Roosevelt believed that this action, on the part of European nations, would threaten the United States and the Western Hemisphere. Therefore, he decided that if a Latin American nation failed to pay its debts or was in conflict with other nations, the United States would become involved. In this case, American representatives were assigned to collect the money and transfer it to the foreign debtors.

As the United States assumed the role as a world power, a canal shortening the distance between the Atlantic and Pacific Oceans became necessary. In 1901 Secretary John Hay secured a treaty which stated that the United States, independently, could build and control an Isthmian canal. Several different routes were investigated, and it was finally decided to develop the Panama route which was located in Colombia. Colombia rejected the treaty offered by the United States. In November 1903, under the protection of United States warships, the Panamanians revolted successfully against Colombia. The United States immediately recognized the new government of Panama and signed a treaty to build the canal. Seven years later, in 1914, the Panama Canal, operated by the United States, was opened to shipping.

President Roosevelt's prestige was acknowledged abroad as well as at home. Russia and Japan were engaged in a war for the possession of Manchuria and Korea. President Roosevelt invited Russia and Japan to meet in Portsmouth, New Hampshire, to discuss the dispute. They attended the conference which eventually resulted in a peace treaty.

President Roosevelt received the Nobel prize, in 1906, for his services in the cause of international peace. American-

Japanese relations deteriorated when the San Francisco Board of Education ordered Japanese-American children to attend a separate school. President Roosevelt was successful in persuading the Board of Education to cancel the order. He then concluded a "Gentlemen's Agreement" with Japan which ended the immigration of Japanese farmers to the United States until 1924.

President Roosevelt's successor was William Howard Taft. At the end of his term, President Roosevelt went to Africa on a safari and then visited Europe where he was received with honor and respect. When he returned to the United States, he discovered that the Americans, too, still regarded him as a hero. He was not pleased with President Taft and his administration. Taft tried to continue Roosevelt's policies, but he lacked Roosevelt's personality and style of working. He supported American business investments in foreign countries. President Taft, nevertheless, received the Republican nomination for presidency. It was thought that Senator La Follette would receive the nomination of the Progressive party, but his supporters left him when they learned that Roosevelt was again interested in the presidency. The Progressive party nominated Theodore Roosevelt for president. Meanwhile, the Democrats nominated Governor Woodrow Wilson of New Jersey for the presidency. The election resulted in a victory for the Democrats.

President Woodrow Wilson, a progressive and former university president, followed Taft; and he emphasized friendship with the Latin American countries. Nevertheless, he sent American troops to the Dominican Republic, Haiti, Cuba, and Mexico. President Wilson, a strong leader, believed the presidency was a public trust. His program, the "New Freedom," supported a return to free competition in industry and full publicity for public affairs.

During Wilson's administration the Federal Reserve system was established which could increase or decrease available money in keeping with the needs of the economy. The Federal Trade Commission, created in 1914, had the authority to order companies to cease to exist if they were found to be involved in harmful practices such as using threats, dishonesty, or bribery. The Clayton Anti-trust Act also limited monopolies in other ways. President Wilson wanted to continue his domestic program of social and economic reforms, but the events in Europe were demanding that his attention be directed to world affairs.

FIGURING OUT CHRONOLOGY

What happened first (F)? What happened last (L)? Place the letter of the sentence in the appropriate blank.

1. (F) _____   a. The United States signs a treaty with the new nation of Panama to build a canal.

                     b. Woodrow Wilson is elected president of the United States for his first term.

    (L) _____   c. Robert La Follette is elected governor of Wisconsin.

2. (F) _____   a. President Wilson appoints Louis Brandeis to the Supreme Court.

                     b. Congress declares war on Spain.

    (L) _____   c. Jane Addams opens Hull House in Chicago.

3. (F) _____   a. President Roosevelt receives the Nobel Peace Prize for his work at the Portsmouth Conference.

                     b. President Roosevelt intervenes in the anthracite coal miners' strike.

    (L) _____   c. William Howard Taft is elected president.

4. (F) _____   a. Woodrow Wilson is elected governor of New Jersey.

                     b. The Panama Canal opens for the traffic of ships.

    (L) _____   c. Theodore Roosevelt becomes vice president of the United States.

5. (F) _____   a. Upton Sinclair publishes his novel, *The Jungle*.

                     b. The Clayton Anti-trust Act passes.

    (L) _____   c. Fire kills workers at the Triangle Shirtwaist Company in New York City.

6. (F) _____   a. The Meat Inspection Act passes.

                     b. The Federal Reserve Act passes.

    (L) _____   c. President McKinley is assassinated.

7. (F) _____   a. The Hepburn Railroad Regulation Act passes.

                     b. The Women's Christian Temperance Union (WCTU) is founded.

    (L) _____   c. President Roosevelt mediates the settlement of the Russo-Japanese War.

8. (F) _____   a. Theodore Roosevelt is elected governor of New York.

                     b. The Panama Canal opens for the traffic of ships.

    (L) _____   c. President Wilson appoints Louis Brandeis to the Supreme Court.

WHAT WOULD YOU HAVE DONE?

Write a short composition explaining your position with supporting evidence on one of the following events:

    a. The peace treaty with the new nation of Panama

    b. The "Gentlemen's Agreement" with Japan

    c. The intervention of the United States in the Dominican Republic's financial affairs

    d. The intervention of President Roosevelt in the anthracite coal miners' strike

_____

_____

_____

_____

_____

_____

_____

_____

_____

_____

_____

_____

_____

_____

_____

_____

_____

_____

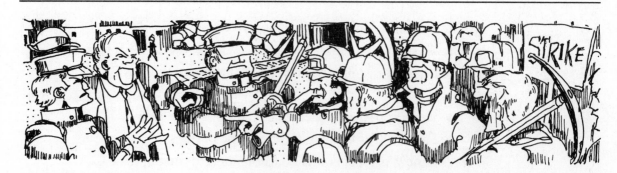

SUGGESTED TEACHING ACTIVITIES

1. Topics for further study:
   a. Theodore Roosevelt
   b. Mark Hanna
   c. J. Pierpont Morgan
   d. John Mitchell
   e. anthracite coal miners' strike
   f. "New Freedom"
   g. conservation
   h. "square deal"
   i. Gifford Pinchot
   j. Panama Canal
   k. Sierra Club
   l. John Muir
   m. William Howard Taft
   n. Woodrow Wilson
   o. Louis Brandeis
   p. Panic of 1907
   q. National Forest Service
   r. George W. Goethals

2. Assign students to prepare a list of at least 10 national parks in the United States. Tell when each was authorized by the government to be a national park, where it is located, the amount of acreage, and the outstanding features of the park. If possible include photographs (post cards) which show some of the scenes in each park. Students may display their findings in the classroom to share with other students.

3. Assign students to describe briefly the provisions of the following legislation and the duties of the system and commission. Also, note when and under whose presidency it was established.
   a. Hepburn Act
   b. Sherman Anti-trust Act
   c. Underwood Tariff
   d. Meat Inspection Act
   e. Clayton Anti-trust Act
   f. Pure Food and Drug Act
   g. Federal Trade Commission
   h. Federal Reserve System

4. Assign student volunteer(s) to prepare a model or drawings of the Panama Canal and to explain how it operates to their classmates. Also, a map showing the Canal Zone, its geographical features, and the route of the canal would help students understand how great an engineering feat this was. A class discussion regarding the display may involve the number of persons who worked on the project and how they were recruited, the cost, and the problems regarding supplies and food as well as sanitation and disease. What were the fees for the use of the canal? How were the fees determined and collected? What are the fees today?

5. Invite a member of the Sierra Club to visit the classroom and speak about the club's environmental work and the contributions of John Muir and Theodore Roosevelt to the club's movement.

6. As a class, prepare a chart on the chalkboard comparing President Theodore Roosevelt, President William Howard Taft, and President Woodrow Wilson. How were the men similar? How were they different? What were the most important achievements in each of the administrations?

7. Class Discussion: Who were the three major candidates for president in the election of 1912? Who won the election and why? If students in class had been able to vote in that election, for which candidate would they have voted and why? What percentage of the popular votes did each candidate get? The electoral votes? Using this data, prepare a graph on the chalkboard. Do you think the outcome was inevitable? Why?

Suggestions for Supplementary Reading:

Garraty, John A. *Theodore Roosevelt: The Strenuous Life*. American Heritage Junior Library. New York: American Heritage Publishing Co., Inc., 1967.

St. George, Judith. *Panama Canal: Gateway to the World*. New York: G. P. Putnam's Sons, 1989.

Tolan, Sally. *John Muir: Naturalist, Writer, and Guardian of the North American Wilderness*. Milwaukee: Gareth Stevens Children's Books, 1990.

THE "WAR TO END WARS"

The Great War began in August 1914 when Austria invaded Serbia in the Balkans. On June 28, 1914, the Archduke Franz Ferdinand, heir to the throne of Austria-Hungary, was assassinated by a Serbian terrorist while visiting in Sarajevo, the capital of Bosnia. This incident, almost insignificant, set off a chain of events that led to a world war. This war provided the setting to challenge and test the powers of Great Britain and Germany. Great Britain had established itself as the world's most powerful nation and Germany challenged that power. The nations of Europe were organized into two groups, or alliances. Each nation within an alliance had agreed to join a member country if that country became involved in a war with an enemy. The Central Powers of Germany, Austria-Hungary, and Turkey formed one alliance. The Allies of Great Britain, France, and Russia formed another alliance.

President Woodrow Wilson believed that the United States should remain neutral, that is, supporting neither side. Many Americans were not neutral. Americans were likely to identify with the nations from which they or their ancestors had come. Even President Wilson was in sympathy with Great Britain, admiring its culture and political system. Because of effective propaganda materials, Americans believed that Germany was aggressive and brutal. The war had caused the greatest economic prosperity in United States history. The role of business made the nation's neutrality doubtful. The United States was developing extensive trade and financial ties with warring nations, providing war materials and food.

The Germans used submarine warfare which many Americans thought was brutal. A submarine could not "visit and search" a ship to protect its crew and passengers before destroying it. Germany promised that its submarines would not attack neutral ships or interfere with neutral shipping. On May 17, 1915, a British ocean liner, the *Lusitania*, was torpedoed off the Irish coast without warning. It sank with the loss of nearly 1,200 lives, including 114 Americans. President Wilson protested but the Germans defended this action because the ship carried guns and ammunition. Americans began to shift away from neutrality toward involvement in the war on the side of the Allies. President Wilson tried to maintain peace. On March 24, 1916, a German submarine torpedoed the French steamer, the *Sussex*, with the loss of American lives. President Wilson again protested. The Germans yielded and drew back.

By the end of Wilson's first term of office, war was the major topic. The Democrats again nominated Wilson for the presidency, and the Republicans nominated Charles E. Hughes. This election proved to be very close. President Wilson returned to office with the campaign slogan, "He Kept Us Out of War."

On April 6, 1917, two weeks after German submarines had torpedoed three American ships, Congress declared war on Germany. Young men were drafted to fight in Europe. Not until the spring of 1918 were American troops, the American Expeditionary Force, there in significant numbers. Eight months later the war was over. Under the command of General John J. Pershing, the American troops helped to halt and then push the Germans back toward their own border, cutting their major supply lines. The German military leaders began to seek an armistice, an agreement to stop fighting. On November 11, 1918, the Great War ended.

To pay for the war, the federal government had appropriated $32 billion for expenses directly related to the war. To raise the money, the government sold "Liberty Bonds" to the public. By 1920 the sale of bonds provided 23 billion dollars. At the same time, new taxes brought in an additional $10 billion. Boards were created to manage the war effort efficiently. The Railroad Administration managed the railroads as one system, making certain that troops, war supplies, and food reached the proper destinations as quickly as possible. The Food Administration, headed by Herbert Hoover, supervised the efforts to provide food for the nation, its armies, and its Allies, all of whom were dependent on American agriculture. The War Industries Board coordinated the manufacture of war goods and the government's purchase of military supplies. The National War Labor Board, established in April 1918, served as a court for labor disputes.

Not everyone was in favor of declaring war. Public opinion had been deeply divided. There were pacifists, people who refuse to fight in war, and isolationists, people who believe in avoiding involvement with other nations, opposed to U.S. participation in the conflict. A propaganda campaign distributed government-promoted films justifying U.S. entry into war. The Espionage Act of 1917 imposed heavy fines and jail terms on those convicted of spying, sabotaging, or obstructing the war effort. About 1,500 people were arrested. People of German ancestry were harassed and fired from their jobs.

President Wilson presented his peace plan before the war ended. The "Fourteen Points" would provide the framework for a just and lasting peace. Wilson's proposals contained specific recommendations for adjusting boundaries and for establishing new nations, all reflecting his belief in the right of all peoples to govern themselves. It also listed general principles, such as freedom of the seas, removal of trade barriers, and orderly disarmament. The fourteenth point, the most important, was Wilson's plan for a peacekeeping organization of nations, the League of Nations.

Wilson attended the Paris Peace Conference. The nations represented at the Conference were not enthusiastic nor supportive of Wilson's proposals. Some of the nations had made secret treaties before the war ended. They felt strongly that Germany should not be allowed to become powerful enough to threaten Europe again. They wanted Germany to pay for the losses and damages. Even in the United States, Wilson had problems in securing congressional approval of the "Fourteen Points."

The Treaty of Versailles was signed on May 7, 1919, imposing harsh measures against Germany. The treaty did not represent Wilson's proposals. However, the League of Nations was established, with its headquarters in Geneva, Switzerland, to help keep peace among the nation members. The United States refused to ratify the treaty and did not join the League of Nations.

Americans, after the Russian Revolution, were disturbed about a Communist threat in this country. They were fearful of "radicals," people who wanted extreme changes in government. In 1920 two Italian immigrants, Nicola Sacco and Bartolomeo Vanzetti, were charged with the murder of a paymaster in Braintree, Massachusetts. The evidence presented was questionable, but both men were confessed anarchists. They were convicted and sentenced to death by a prejudiced judge. Requests for a new trial or pardon were denied. In 1927 they died, still insisting upon their innocence.

Increasing economic problems and widespread social unrest and violence were becoming evident in America. The economy began to falter; farmers lost their land and workers lost their jobs. The Seattle shipyard workers, the Boston police force, and the steelworkers went on strike. They were powerless. Black Americans who had moved to the cities for factory work were treated unfairly. Competition for jobs and discrimination led to violence and riots in the large cities. Marcus Garvey encouraged blacks to take pride in their own achievements and heritage. He urged them to return to Africa and create a new society of their own. Most blacks, though, had no choice but to accept life in America as it was until more progress could be made toward equality for all.

CONNECTING WORDS AND DEFINITIONS

Match the item in Column 1 with its description in Column 2.

Column 1	Column 2
_____1. pacifist	a. A person who advocates abolishing all forms of government.
_____2. anarchist	b. A person whose political beliefs tend to favor change, reform of inequalities, and an active role for the federal government.
_____3. isolationist	c. A person who refuses to bear arms or serve in the military forces because of religious beliefs and principles.
_____4. idealist	d. A person who believes in the established way of doing things and who does not like to see changes. This person tends to favor individual initiative, unregulated marketplace, and minimum government involvement in social welfare.
_____5. realist	e. A person who opposes the use of force under any circumstances and refuses to participate in war or any military action.
_____6. liberal	f. A person who believes in saving and managing natural resources for the benefit of all people.
_____7. conservative	g. A person who is concerned with real things and practical matters rather than imaginary ones and who sees the world as it really is.
_____8. progressive	h. A person who refuses to become generally involved in world affairs and avoids alliances with other nations.
_____9. conservationist	i. A person who looks at the world and sees things as they should be or as one would wish them to be and whose behavior and thinking are based on this perception of the world.
_____10. conscientious objector	j. A person who works actively for progress and reform in society.

Name_____

LIFE CAN BE EXCITING!

If you were given the opportunity to live during the administration of President Theodore Roosevelt (1901–1909) *or* President Woodrow Wilson (1913–1921), which one would you select? Write a short composition telling why you selected that period of time in United States history. Also, note in your composition how old you are, what career you are pursuing, your friends, your contacts with government, your activities, and any other relevant information.

_____

_____

_____

_____

_____

_____

_____

_____

_____

_____

_____

_____

_____

_____

_____

_____

_____

_____

_____

_____

SUGGESTED TEACHING ACTIVITIES

1. Topics for further study:
   a. Colonel Edward House
   b. Woodrow Wilson
   c. Edith Cavell
   d. Bernard Baruch
   e. black Americans in war
   f. Fourteen Points
   g. U-boats
   h. pacifists
   i. Herbert Hoover
   j. Nineteenth Amendment
   k. doughboys
   l. League of Nations
   m. *Lusitania*
   n. anarchists
   o. *Sussex*
   p. Selective Service Act
   q. General John J. Pershing
   r. Senator Henry Cabot Lodge

2. Assign students to write a short report about one of the following wives of presidents: Alice Lee Roosevelt (died while Roosevelt was governor of New York), Edith Kermit Roosevelt, Helen Herron Taft, Ellen Axson Wilson (died while Wilson was president), or Edith Bolling Wilson. Tell something about the woman and how she influenced her husband. How did she view her role as first lady? How does she compare with the first ladies of today?

3. Congress passed the Espionage Act of 1917 which imposed heavy fines and jail terms on those convicted of spying, sabotaging, or obstructing the war effort. The following year, the Sabotage Act and Sedition Act were passed which made any public expression of opposition to war illegal. Conscientious objectors, those people who refused to serve in the military because of their religious beliefs, were imprisoned. Assign student volunteers to find out why the following people were convicted: Eugene V. Debs, "Red Emma" Goldman, and "Big Bill" Haywood. Class Discussion: Do you think that the federal government should have the right to limit freedom of speech and religion (Constitutional guarantees) during wartime? Students should provide supporting evidence for their views.

4. A student volunteer may report orally about the Arlington National Cemetery located in Virginia and the monument at the Tomb of the Unknown American Soldier of World War I.

5. Students may prepare special reports on Henry Ford and the peace ship which sailed, in December 1915, to Europe to hold a series of peace meetings. Henry Ford pledged the funding for the trip and Jane Addams of Hull House led the "peace pilgrims." How successful were the efforts of this group? Explain. Barbara S. Kraft's book entitled *The Peace Ship* provides pertinent information about the venture.

6. Prepare a time line to include the following events:
   a. Austrian invasion of Serbia
   b. Execution of Sacco and Vanzetti
   c. Death of Woodrow Wilson
   d. Treaty of Versailles signed
   e. Sedition Act passed
   f. Armistice ends the war
   g. *Lusitania* torpedoed
   h. President Wilson reelected

7. Students may prepare special reports on Nicola Sacco and Bartolomeo Vanzetti, Italian immigrants who were convicted of murder and executed in the electric chair. Why were they convicted? Were they guilty? Explain. Do you think they were victims of fear and prejudice? Explain. Do you think that capital punishment was appropriate in this case? In any case? Why?

AGE OF PROSPERITY AND CHANGE

The beginning of the 1920s found the United States facing problems in adjusting to its political, industrial, and social life. Americans were strong and confident that they could deal with them. Presidents like Theodore Roosevelt and Woodrow Wilson, strong and aggressive leaders, had brought the government nearer to the people. Government was engaged in all kinds of activities and programs such as helping the needy, international cooperation, production and distribution of manufactured goods, and industrial regulation. Congress was now in session for many more weeks, and the debates were more widely publicized among interested citizens.

Warren G. Harding of Ohio was elected to the presidency in 1920. He campaigned from the front porch of his home in Ohio and promised to "return to normalcy." People wanted life to be as it was before the war. He was also the first president to speak to the people over the radio. He believed it was the responsibility of the federal government to help businesses and corporations succeed in the economy. He was a pleasant person with little experience for the presidency. When he assumed the presidency, he appointed Charles Evans Hughes, Herbert Hoover, and Andrew W. Mellon. These men were highly qualified and competent. Some of the other appointments were disappointing. One of his appointments as Secretary of the Interior was Albert Fall. The government had reserve oil fields in Teapot Dome, Wyoming, and Elk Hills, California. Albert Fall leased these two government reserve oil fields to private interests in return for gifts and loans. This transaction became known as The Teapot Dome scandal. Fall was convicted of bribery. President Harding did not possess a strong leadership to control the dishonesty, bribery, and corruption during his administration. While in office, President Harding pardoned socialist Eugene V. Debs in 1921.

Vice President Calvin Coolidge was an interesting man, very different from President Harding. When President Harding died suddenly before the end of his term, Vice President Calvin Coolidge was in Vermont with his family. Coolidge's father administered the oath of presidential office to him. He was known as "Silent Cal." As a quiet and honest man, he supported business and believed that government should not interfere with what business wanted to do. The majority of the voters seemed willing to go along with this policy. In the election of 1924, Coolidge was successful in his bid for the presidency. Andrew Mellon and Herbert Hoover served competently in his cabinet. Herbert Hoover became the Republican presidential candidate in the election of 1928, and he defeated Alfred Smith, the Democratic candidate.

During the 1920s the United States experienced prosperity and economic growth. There was a need for American manufactured products and food in devastated Europe until life returned to normal. The development of the automobile by Henry Ford was an important event which aided in economic growth and caused changes in American life. The introduction of the assembly line made the manufacturing of automobiles efficient and the cost more reasonable. In 1921 Americans bought one and a half million automobiles; in 1929 they purchased five million automobiles. To make automobiles, the manufacturers needed steel, glass, tools, machines, and other products. This led to the development and growth of related industries and services. People who owned automobiles needed gasoline and roads on which to drive. Gasoline stations and road construction companies developed. Home construction increased since the automobile allowed people to build homes further from their places of work. The radio industry, motion picture industry, aviation, electronics, and home appliances were developing. Companies that were dependent on large-scale mass production were consolidating to promote efficiency and created large corporations. People were shopping in national chain stores rather than locally owned shops.

The economic growth was remarkable. At the same time, the wealth and purchasing power of the people were unequally distributed. It is estimated that about two thirds of the Americans in 1929 lived at the minimum comfort level. Nevertheless, American workers saw their standard of living rise, and they did enjoy improved working conditions and other benefits. Many people earned enough money to improve their lives.

A few employers who wanted to avoid labor problems and the growth of labor unions adopted "welfare capitalism." Henry Ford shortened the work week and gave paid vacations to his employees. In some companies, employees received increases in their wages, improved sanitation and safety in the workplace, and retirement pensions. However, the owners did not offer employees any job security. The unskilled workers labored for low wages and they were powerless to do anything about it. The American Federation of Labor had no interest in organizing unskilled workers who were mainly immigrants, women, and black Americans. They were reluctant to call strikes. Unions were accused of being subversive organizations which were attempting, secretly, to overthrow the American government. Employers advocated the open shop, a workplace where no worker could be required to join a union. The decisions of the Supreme Court did not help the cause of unions. One of the decisions made picketing an illegal activity.

The farmers, during the 1920s, experienced a continued downtrend in their income. Like the industrialists, the farmers used technology to increase production which was needed for the huge consumer demand. As Europe's economy improved, they purchased less and less food from Americans. The food consumed by Americans remained about the same. Consequently, agricultural expansion caused serious problems in food prices and a drop in farm income. During the 1920s three million people left the farms. Farmers wanted government assistance in controlling and stabilizing prices of food products.

During the 1920s the United States became a consumer society. Wealthy and ordinary Americans could afford to buy products that were necessary and some which were just enjoyable to have. Appliances such as electric refrigerators and washing machines changed the way families lived and managed their homes. The automobile, as it became affordable, was in great demand as a means of transportation and enjoyment. Advertisements in newspapers, magazines, and on radio encouraged consumers to buy products such as processed foods, cosmetics, household appliances, and many others that the modern economy produced. The radio provided entertainment, too, and encouraged the development of sports as a national pastime. People were informed about happenings almost instantly.

The culture of the 1920s affected women in several ways. Some women were college-educated. Career opportunities were still limited although it was now possible for women to have both a marriage and a career. Women became more active in political activities. With modern technology, women experienced a significant increase in their leisure time. The modern woman of the 1920s expressed her freedom by the way she dressed, her hair style, her dance, and her speech. Nevertheless, women realized that their "freedom" was being resisted. Some reform movements encouraged the establishment of women's organizations such as the League of Women Voters. Women's campaign for equal rights made little progress during the 1920s. Women activists were able to get Congress to pass the Sheppard-Towner Act which provided prenatal and health care programs for children. In 1929 this program was ended.

Education was an important part of society and the family. More young people were enrolled in high schools. The schools offered a variety of programs, not only the traditional academic curriculum. They provided training in areas such as the new technical skills, engineering, and economics. Since young people had to spend more time in training before entering the workplace, the "adolescent culture" began to emerge. Adolescents identified themselves more and more with their peer groups rather than their families. Schools also developed extra-curricular activities such as clubs and organized sports. Thomas Edison, Henry Ford, and Charles Lindbergh were highly admired heroes who had become popular without the benefit of formal education. Nevertheless, the "self-made man" of Horatio Alger's time was disappearing.

The Eighteenth Amendment, which prohibited the manufacture and sale of alcoholic beverages, went into effect on January 20, 1920. The Volstead Act was passed over President Wilson's veto to go into effect on the same day. This law defined an intoxicating beverage as one that contained at least one-half of one percent of alcohol. Individuals violated the law, and as time went on, the violations grew to include members of organized crime. Not much money was provided for federal agents to enforce the prohibition laws. Therefore, organized crime was able to take control of manufacturing, selling, and distributing illegal alcohol. The law was ineffective. It was not until 1933 that the Eighteenth Amendment was repealed.

The Ku Klux Klan had been ineffective since the middle 1870s; however, it had a new beginning in the 1920s as it began to spread to industrial cities in the North. Membership was restricted to white, American-born Protestant men. They terrorized minorities—blacks, Jews, Catholics, and foreigners—and tried to force them out of their communities. Their influence began to decline by the mid 1920s.

In 1924 Congress passed the National Origins Act which set lower quotas for southern and eastern European immigrants and prohibited all immigration from Asia. This Act was promoted by the nativists who were prejudiced against immigrants. The Asians felt offended and insulted by this Act. Immigration from Canada or Latin America was not restricted. The quotas or the numbers of immigrants allowed to come to the United States were based on the "national origin" of the people residing in the United States during the 1890 census when there were more western and northern Europeans in the population. The total number of immigrants was reduced to 164,000 a year. In 1929 the number of immigrants allowed to enter was decreased to 150,000.

By the end of the 1920s America was a much different place from what it had been before the war. Changes occurred at a faster rate than ever before. The American way of living with the products of technology, the ideas Americans believed, and the values they upheld was changing.

THE ARTS IN THE 1920s

The artists and writers of the 1920s were unhappy with the direction in which American society was moving. They believed there was too much emphasis on materialism. Nevertheless, Sinclair Lewis, F. Scott Fitzgerald, and Ernest Hemingway emerged as outstanding writers of that decade. Many American artists and writers left the United States to live in France. Paris became the center of creative activities for Americans. Eugene O'Neill was the first American playwright to win a Nobel Prize. The American writers were creative and experimental in different ways which were effective. Many artists and writers encouraged reform and change. Some of them began using their regional or cultural origins as subjects for their creative products. Black artists and writers were a part of the "Harlem Renaissance" which drew themes from their own heritage for their creative works. Langston Hughes, a black poet, wrote "I am a Negro—and beautiful." William Faulkner, an outstanding author, also drew from his heritage to write his novels about the South. These were the years of jazz music and silent films. Many outstanding musicians and performers such as Louis Armstrong, Ethel Waters, Will Rogers, and Charlie Chaplin were entertaining audiences.

List at least three artists of the 1920s; they may be artists, writers, musicians, or film and stage performers. Tell something about their lives, briefly describe their work, and then explain how they influenced American life.

ARTIST	EXAMPLES OF THEIR WORK	INFLUENCE ON AMERICAN LIFE
1. _____	_____	_____
	_____	_____
	_____	_____
	_____	_____
	_____	_____
2. _____	_____	_____
	_____	_____
	_____	_____
	_____	_____
	_____	_____
3. _____	_____	_____
	_____	_____
	_____	_____
	_____	_____
	_____	_____

THE AUTOMOBILE CHANGES AMERICAN LIFE

New technological advances affected the lives of Americans in the 1920s. The automobile and the assembly-line method of manufacturing were probably the most important developments which caused great changes in many different aspects of life. The assembly line was so efficient that the price of the automobile was reduced, making it affordable to many Americans.

List at least 10 changes in American life caused by the automobile.

_____

_____

_____

_____

_____

_____

_____

_____

_____

_____

Then, select at least two of the changes and note the development of related services, industries, and problems that were created by the changes and how they were resolved.

_____

_____

_____

_____

_____

_____

_____

_____

_____

_____

_____

_____

1. Topics for further study:
   a. Warren G. Harding
   b. Teapot Dome
   c. Charles Evans Hughes
   d. Herbert Hoover
   e. Andrew W. Mellon
   f. Calvin Coolidge
   g. Alfred Smith
   h. Henry Ford
   i. sewing machine
   j. refrigerator
   k. farmers in the 1920s
   l. Eighteenth Amendment
   m. National Origins Act
   n. Ku Klux Klan
   o. John T. Scopes
   p. Clarence Darrow
   q. Charles Darwin
   r. Charles Lindbergh

2. Assign students to study the presidential elections of 1920, 1924, and 1928. A chart could be prepared which includes the names of all candidates and their parties, short biographical sketch of each candidate, the main issues in the party platform, and the winner.

3. During the late 1920s jazz could be heard everywhere in the United States. Bring to class recordings by jazz musicians such as Louis Armstrong and "blues singers" like Gertrude "Ma" Rainey, Bessie Smith, and others and play the recordings for the class. How and why did jazz music develop? What does jazz music tell about the 1920s?

4. During the Scopes trial, the basic issue was between science and religion. Were human beings descended from monkeys, or were they made from clay and Adam's rib? Bring to class copies of Jerome Lawrence and Robert E. Lee's *Inherit the Wind*. Selected excerpts of this play can be read aloud by the students. It is interesting and students will enjoy reading the lines during the highly dramatic and witty scenes. How did the views of the two lawyers differ? Prepare a chart on the chalkboard, showing the differences. What techniques were used by the lawyers? How effective were they? A video of *Inherit the Wind* is also available and can be shown to the class.

5. Women had earned the right to vote when the Nineteenth Amendment to the Constitution was passed in 1920. Class Discussion: What changes occurred with the passage of the Nineteenth Amendment? Did this amendment also guarantee equal rights for women? The Equal Rights Amendment was first proposed by the National Women's Party in 1923. What were the provisions of the Equal Rights Amendment? Has this amendment passed? Why or why not? Would you support this amendment if it were presented again? Why?

6. Assign students to prepare a time line to include the following events:
   a. Charles Lindbergh's transatlantic flight
   b. Warren G. Harding elected president
   c. Herbert Hoover elected president
   d. Teapot Dome scandal revealed
   e. The Scopes Trial
   f. Sacco and Vanzetti Trial
   g. Sinclair Lewis published *Babbitt*
   h. Death of President Harding
   i. Passage of Nineteenth Amendment
   j Passage of the Eighteenth Amendment
   k. Calvin Coolidge elected president
   l. *The Jazz Singer*, film, released
   m. National Origins Act passed
   n. First commercial radio broadcast in Pittsburgh

7. During the 1920s the United States became a consumer society. The advertising industry assumed a definite role and saw itself important in the development and growth of the economy. Assign students to compare advertisements in a 1920s Sears and Roebuck Catalog and a 1990 Sears Catalog. What are the differences? What are the similarities? Do you agree that the advertising industry is an important part of our economy? Why or why not?

THE GREAT DEPRESSION

Americans had experienced economic depressions, but the Great Depression of the 1930s was different. It lasted longer, it was harsher, and it affected more people. Unemployment was high. Even people with jobs worked for low wages and reduced hours, uncertain whether the job would be there the next day. Farmers lost their lands and sought jobs where none existed. Local and state governments, churches, and other private institutions were unable to cope with the many problems caused by the Great Depression. People expected the federal government to find solutions to the problems. President Hoover developed some innovative programs, but they were not enough.

The stock market crash in October 1929, known as "Black Thursday," was a momentous day in American history. Farmers, laborers, and others did not have enough money to purchase the goods on the market. As businesses made greater profits in the 1920s, they did not share those profits with laborers through increases in wages. There was not enough demand for products and the surpluses increased. Factories were forced to close, causing unemployment. European nations were also experiencing financial problems, and they could not afford to buy from Americans nor repay their war debts. The stock market itself provided speculation, and people lost their confidence in the nation's economy.

Production decreased, farm prices fell dramatically, and unemployment increased. Families were forced to seek relief in bread lines and soup kitchens. The situation in rural areas was even worse. Blacks and Hispanics found life during the depression even more depressing and humiliating. They were generally the last to be hired and the first to be fired. Other Americans showed very little sensitivity to their poverty, often demanding that employers replace them with "white Americans." In some cases women were the sole breadwinners in a family.

Many people felt that the problems of the depression were the fault of society rather than of individuals. Many artists and writers expressed this view in their writings, paintings, and photography.

When Herbert Hoover became president, he did not know what problems were ahead. He was urged to support innovative and vigorous programs for relief and public spending which he ignored. President Hoover continued to make optimistic statements and unrealistic comments about the American economy. The most important legislation during his administration was the establishment of the Reconstruction Finance Corporation. This agency was to provide federal loans

to banks and businesses. It provided financial assistance to local governments to support public works and projects. However, it was not enough to ease the effects of the depression. Six months after the stock market crash, more than 4 million people were out of work. By the beginning of the winter of 1931, unemployment had reached 8 million.

Farmers were not only suffering because of the economic depression but also because of a natural disaster. In the summer of 1930, a drought, which lasted almost 10 years, dried up the farmlands. The "Dust Bowl" included 19 states, mostly in the Great Plains. With mechanization, farmers produced more than they could sell at reasonable prices. Consequently, the prices fell. The farmers were heavily in debt as they mortgaged their farms. President Hoover urged the farmers to plant less so that the prices for their produce would increase. However, they did not heed his advice. The farmers organized, developed a program, and marched to Washington to present it to the Congress. They wanted cash relief administered by a committee of farmers. Their proposals were rejected. When they were unable to meet their mortgage payments, they left their farms. Many farmers became seasonal pickers and migrant workers.

After the first World War, Congress passed a bill to pay veterans of that war bonuses in 1945. In 1932 a group of jobless and starving veterans met in Oregon to form the Bonus Expeditionary Force and asked that the bonuses be paid immediately. The men decided to go to Washington, D. C., to pressure Congress to pass the Patman Bill which proposed immediate payment of a veteran's bonus. They began with a few men; but, by the time they reached Washington, D. C., there were about 15,000 veterans and their families. They camped near the White House in shanties and makeshift dwellings on Anacostia Flats in the southeast corner of Washington, D. C. Congress did not approve the bill to provide payment of the bonuses. Many of the veterans and their families did not know what to do next. President Hoover felt they were a threat to American government and a reminder of the poverty experienced by unfortunate Americans. He ordered them to leave and the Army Chief of Staff, Douglas MacArthur, to use federal troops to drive them away.

In the election of 1932, President Hoover was again nominated as the presidential candidate of the Republicans. Franklin Delano Roosevelt, the Democratic candidate, won. President Hoover's lack of popularity among the masses of people and the condition of the economy made it possible for Roosevelt to win by a landslide. Just a month before his inauguration, the American banking system began to collapse. Roosevelt had inherited an administration beset with serious economic, social, and political problems.

FINDING CONNECTIONS

Connect the items in Column I with their descriptions in Column 2.

Column 1

_____ 1. President Calvin Coolidge

_____ 2. Bonus March

_____ 3. welfare

_____ 4. mortgage

_____ 5. "Dust Bowl"

_____ 6. President Herbert Hoover

_____ 7. bonus

_____ 8. Reconstruction Finance Corporation

_____ 9. October 24, Black Thursday

_____ 10. decade

_____ 11. weakness in economy

_____ 12. Hoovervilles

_____ 13. Okies

Column 2

a. Shantytowns established by the homeless on the outskirts of cities.

b. He believed that government should not be in the business of providing direct relief and assistance for individuals.

c. Families who abandoned their farms in the "Dust Bowl" area and migrated to California to find a better life.

d. A period of 10 years.

e. He made a decision while in office not to seek reelection.

f. A payment made by the government to veterans of military service.

g. An area in the United States that experienced a severe drought. The land became so dry that the topsoil became dust.

h. A protest movement by veterans of the first World War who wanted their bonuses in 1932, not in 1945.

i. State and/or federal programs that provide food, money, medical care, and other help to those who are jobless and homeless.

j. When borrowing money, to provide the bank or lender a claim on one's property if the debt is not repaid when it is due.

k. Authorized to lend money to banks and to businesses to keep them in operation.

l. Even as production increased during the 1920s, the wages of laborers did not keep pace with the increase in profits.

m. Day of stock market crash on Wall Street.

UNEMPLOYMENT

Make a bar graph showing the percentage of the civilian labor force who were unemployed between 1920 and 1930. Use the following data:

UNEMPLOYMENT: From 1920-1940 (in thousands of persons 14 years old and over)					
YEAR	NUMBER OF UNEMPLOYED	% OF CIVILIAN LABOR FORCE	YEAR	NUMBER OF UNEMPLOYED	% OF CIVILIAN LABOR FORCE
1940	8,120	14.6	1930	4,340	8.7
1939	9,480	17.2	1929	1,550	3.2
1938	10,390	19.0	1928	1,982	4.2
1937	7,700	14.3	1927	1,519	3.3
1936	9,030	16.9	1926	801	1.8
1935	10,610	20.1	1925	1,453	3.2
1934	11,340	21.7	1924	2,190	5.0
1933	12,830	24.9	1923	1,049	2.4
1932	12,060	23.6	1922	2,859	6.7
1931	8,020	15.9	1921	4,918	11.7
			1920	2,132	5.2

BAR GRAPH:

What inferences can you make regarding unemployment during this period of time? Why did it increase? Why did it decrease?

_____

_____

_____

SUGGESTED TEACHING ACTIVITIES

1. Suggested topics for further study:
   a. President Herbert Hoover
   b. Franklin Delano Roosevelt
   c. stock market crash
   d. Dorothea Lange

   e. John Steinbeck
   f. migrant workers, Okies
   g. Dust Bowl
   h. Thomas Hart Benton

   i. Anacostia Flats
   j. soup kitchens
   k. Hoovervilles
   l. Alexander Hogue

2. Read to the class the book by Angela Shelf Medearis entitled *Picking Peas for a Penny* (drawings by Charles Shaw) Austin, TX: State House Press, 1990). This is a book for young students but will be appreciated by older students. It is a lyrical counting rhyme and biographical poem about the experiences that the author's mother and uncle had during the depression. A black girl (mother of the author) describes the difficult work involved in growing up on a farm during the depression. What keeps the family working together in the field of peas? Is this a "hard-times tale"? Explain. Do you think the depression was more serious on the farms or in the cities? Explain.

3. Assign students to interview people in their family and/or communities who experienced the Great Depression. Before the interview, have students list the questions that might be asked during such an interview. Also, discuss how to interview a person and list the points on the chalkboard, such as being courteous, asking clear questions which do not demand a yes or no answer, listening, using a tape recorder, or getting biographical data about person being interviewed.

4. Have students imagine that they are reporters for a newspaper and have been following the veterans from Oregon to Washington, D. C. They have witnessed the meetings and conflicts at Anacostia Flats and the sessions in Congress where veterans discussed the bonus question. Assign them to write one article and one editorial about any event relating to the veterans and their problems.

5. Map Study: Assign students to locate the "Dust Bowl" on a map of the United States. How many states were included? What did the dust storms do to the land? How did the drought affect the people in that area? What is the condition of the land today? If someone in your family lived in one of those states, find out how they were affected during the dust storms.

6. Read and discuss excerpts from John Steinbeck's book entitled *The Grapes of Wrath*. This is a powerful story about migrant workers. The videotape of the film may be shown to the class.

7. Assign students to write a short paper and/or poem about their feelings. Imagine that you and your family are standing in a bread line waiting for some food. Your father has not had a job for at least one year. How do you feel physically as you stand in line? Emotionally? Explain. Do you think that people in the 1930s had the same feelings as you think you would? Students may make arrangements to volunteer their help in a soup kitchen in the community. (Contact the Salvation Army, a church group, or other community group.)

8. Assign students to visit an art museum and to identify a painting, sculpture, or photograph related to the period of the Great Depression. Write a short paper describing the art object and how it communicates the ideas of the artist relating to the depression and a short biographical summary of the artist.

THE NEW DEAL

Franklin Delano Roosevelt was nominated for the presidency at the 1932 Democratic Convention. In his acceptance speech, he said, "I pledge you, I pledge myself, to a new deal for the American people." He said what Americans wanted to hear; he gave them hope. And they gave him the vote and the presidency. In his inaugural speech, his words—"the only thing we have to fear is fear itself" — became a sign for action against the Great Depression. "Try something. If it works, keep doing it. If it doesn't, try something else."

Within two days of assuming office, President Roosevelt ordered the closing of the banks for four days. Three days later Congress passed the Emergency Banking Act. After a governmental inspection, the banks reopened. The president told the American public during one of his many fireside chats it was safe to use the banks, and they did. The crisis was over.

President Roosevelt submitted a number of proposals to Congress to stop the depression from becoming worse. The Agricultural Adjustment Act, passed in May 1933, helped to increase farm prices. It provided for the reduction of crops to eliminate surpluses. The government told the farmers how much they should plant and then paid them for leaving some of their land idle. A tax on food processing provided the money to pay the farmers. The Supreme Court, in January 1936, declared the Agricultural Adjustment Act unconstitutional. The Soil Conservation and Domestic Allotment Act, passed in 1936, made provisions for the government to pay farmers to reduce their crop production to conserve the soil. The Rural Electrification Administration, created in 1935, made electric power available to rural families for the first time.

The National Industrial Recovery Act was passed by Congress in June 1933. It developed codes of fairness to be observed between business and labor to maintain adequate prices and wages. It also set working standards and assigned how much could be manufactured of particular goods and at what price. It was now legal for workers to organize into unions. The Public Works Administration, under the leadership of Interior Secretary Harold L. Ickes, was to be a spending program. Under this program, schools, post offices, bridges, hospitals, and many other public needs were to be constructed and/or renovated. In May 1935, the Supreme Court ruled the NRA unconstitutional. The Tennessee Valley Authority (TVA) was a public regional project, created in May 1933, to develop the nation's water resources as a source of cheap electric power. This project eliminated flooding in the area and provided electricity to thousands of people who had never had it.

The Glass-Steagall Act of June 1933 established the Federal Deposit Insurance Corporation which guaranteed all bank deposits up to $5,000. The Federal Reserve Board with seven members in Washington controlled interest rates. To protect investors, the Truth in Securities Act of 1933 was passed. It required corporations issuing new securities to register them and to provide complete and accurate information.

Roosevelt established the Federal Emergency Relief Administration (FERA), administered by Harry Hopkins, which provided cash grants to states to help bankrupt relief agencies. The Civil Works Administration found work for more than four million people in temporary construction projects. The important thing was that these projects provided money for people to spend, stimulating the economy. It provided assistance to people who had nowhere else to go. The Civilian Conservation Corps provided employment to

young men who could find no jobs. It was intended, at the same time, to advance the work of conservation and reforestation. CCC camps were created in national parks and forests. Young men planted trees, built reservoirs, developed parks, and improved agricultural irrigation. Assistance was provided to farmers in danger of losing their land. Home Owners' Loan Corporation loaned money to refinance the mortgages of more than one million householders. A year later the Federal Housing Administration insured mortgages for the construction of new homes.

Even though President Roosevelt enjoyed great popularity, there were many who criticized the New Deal. One group was the Liberty League, led by the DuPont family. Dr. Francis E. Townsend, a Californian physician, advocated a plan for federal pensions for the elderly. Americans over the age of 60 would receive a monthly pension of $200 if they retired and spent all the money. This idea eventually led to support of the Social Security system, which Congress approved in 1935. Father Charles E. Coughlin, another opponent of the New Deal, supported monetary reforms to restore prosperity.

Because of his critics, President Roosevelt redirected his programs on a new set of ideas known as the "Second New Deal" in 1935. When the National Industrial Recovery Act was declared unconstitutional, the National Labor Relations Act (Wagner Act) was passed. This law guaranteed workers the right to organize and bargain collectively and offered more than the NIRA. It specifically outlawed certain "unfair practices" which employers used in fighting unionization. The Wagner Act also created a National Labor Relations Board to police employers and, if necessary, to force them to recognize and bargain with organized unions.

Workers were unhappy with the conditions in the workplace and began looking toward unionism for a solution. The American Federation of Labor, under William Green, was committed to the idea of organizing workers on the basis of their skills or crafts. Unskilled workers, the majority of the industrial force, needed an organization to help them. John L. Lewis was the dynamic leader of the United Mine Workers, the oldest major union organized by industry rather than craft. He believed that all workers in a particular industry should be organized in a single union, regardless of what functions the workers performed. For instance, all automobile workers should be in a single automobile union. Through the efforts of John L. Lewis, the Congress of Industrial Organization was established in 1936, and he became the first president. This organization included in its membership women and blacks and organized industries such as textiles, laundries, tobacco factories, and others. Sit-down strikes were used effectively to achieve their goals. Employees in automobile plants simply sat down inside the plants, refusing to work or to leave, thus preventing the company from bringing in strikebreakers.

During the General Motors sit-down strike, the government did not intervene on behalf of the employers. The company had no choice but to negotiate with the union. In February 1937, General Motors became the first major manufacturer to recognize the United Automobile Workers. When strikes were called, men and women participated. In 1937 there were about 4,700 strikes called; at least 80 percent of them were settled in favor of the unions. The organization battles of the 1930s established the labor movement as a powerful force in the American economy.

In 1935 the Social Security Act was passed. It provided assistance for the elderly and for American workers. Workers and their employers would contribute to a pension system by paying a payroll tax. On retirement, the worker would receive an income. Certain categories of workers, generally those employing women and blacks, were excluded from the program. Social Security also provided for a system of unemployment insurance, and it established federal aid to disabled people and dependent children.

In 1935 the Works Progress Administration established a system of work relief for the unemployed. Under the direction of Harry Hopkins, public buildings were built or renovated, such as schools and post offices. At the same time, airports, roads, and bridges were constructed. The WPA offered unemployed writers and artists financial support to pursue creative endeavors and to work on public projects. Incomes to those workers employed helped to stimulate the economy by increasing the flow of money in the marketplace. The WPA is regarded as one of the most important pieces of welfare in the history of the United States.

In the presidential election of 1936 President Roosevelt won overwhelmingly. His opponents tried unsuccessfully to establish a new party. Since much of the New Deal legislation was declared unconstitutional by the Supreme Court, President Roosevelt wanted to increase the number of Supreme Court justices. He received criticism for trying to "pack the court." Eventually, the decisions of the Supreme Court became more favorable to the New Deal. Also, as the judges retired, he made his own appointments to the Supreme Court. A slight economic recession occurred in 1937. Historians believe that the New Deal did not bring an end to the depression but that the preparation for war in Europe did.

President Roosevelt was sympathetic to the cause of racial justice. Mrs. Eleanor Roosevelt resigned her membership to the Daughters of the American Revolution when they refused to allow Marian Anderson, a black singer, to sing in their auditorium. The president's wife made arrangements for her to sing on the steps of the Lincoln Memorial. President Roosevelt appointed Robert William Hastie, Mary McLeod Bethune, and others to government offices. African Americans were not excluded in the New Deal programs. The CCC, though, established separate camps for African Americans, and the NRA ignored the fact that they were paid less than whites for doing the same work. Nevertheless, they supported President Roosevelt.

John Collier, commissioner of Indian Affairs, helped to pass the Indian Reorganization Act of 1934. This act returned political authority to the tribes, including the right to form tribal governments and draft tribal constitutions. Government funds were used to support education, health care, and cultural activities. Most importantly, it restored to the tribes the right to own land collectively. These policies were helpful to the the Native Americans; nevertheless, they fell far short of solving some of the serious problems.

President Roosevelt had appointed Secretary of Labor Frances Perkins and named more than 1,200 other women to positions in the federal government. Eleanor Roosevelt was committed to women's rights. The New Deal established a new pattern in American politics. Individual interest groups such as the African Americans, Native Americans, women, Hispanics, and small business owners were learning to organize themselves to demand assistance from the government.

As a part of the New Deal, government spending proved to be important in overcoming an economic depression. Corporations still maintained power, but others, such as farmers and workers, were now able to challenge that power. President Roosevelt enhanced the power of the federal government and challenged the power of Congress. By the end of the 1930s the Democratic party emerged as one of tremendous strength.

NEW DEAL LEGISLATION

For each of the selected New Deal legislation, note the purpose and if it was declared unconstitutional, note why.

1. Agricultural Adjustment Administration (AAA–1933)

2. Tennessee Valley Authority (TVA–1933)

3. Rural Electrification Administration (REA–1935)

4. National Recovery Administration (NRA–1933)

5. Civilian Conservation Corps (CCC–1933)

6. Civil Works Administration (CWA–1933)

7. Public Works Administration (PWA–1933)

8. Works Progress Administration (WPA–1935)

9. National Youth Administration (NYA–1935)

10. Social Security Act (1935)

11. National Labor Relations Act (NLRA–1935)

PEOPLE ARE IMPORTANT

Match the descriptions with the individual.

_____1. Franklin Delano Roosevelt

_____2. Mary McLeod Bethune

_____3. Harry Hopkins

_____4. Eleanor Roosevelt

_____5. Amelia Earhart

_____6. Dr. Francis E. Townsend

_____7. Father Charles Coughlin

_____8. John L. Lewis

_____9. Frances Perkins

_____10. Harold L. Ickes

_____11. Huey Long

a. He called himself the "Kingfish" and served as governor of Louisiana and then as United States senator. He had great political power and developed "Share Our Wealth." He was assassinated in September 1935 at the Louisiana capitol in Baton Rouge.

b. He made regular Sunday radio broadcasts. He accused President Roosevelt of being a friend of the wealthy and an enemy of the poor. He believed the answer to the depression was government ownership of banks, utilities, and natural resources.

c. She was a noted expert in labor relations. President Roosevelt appointed her as his secretary of labor, the first woman Cabinet member. She helped to form the Social Security Act and Fair Labor Standards Act.

d. He was a former social worker who became one of President Roosevelt's closest advisers. He was in charge of organizing the Civil Works Administration program. Later, he helped in planning the United Nations.

e. He was a man of heroic character and appealing personality who loved politics and as president used his position of leadership to provide a better life for everyone.

f. When her husband was crippled with polio, she became his closest partner and political stand-in. She held press conferences, had her own radio program, and wrote a daily newspaper column.

g. He was appointed by President Roosevelt as secretary of the interior. He was the head of the Public Works Administration which created new public project jobs for the jobless.

h. He and seven other union leaders organized the Congress of Industrial Organizations in 1935. He was elected as the first president.

i. She was a member of the "Black Cabinet" who advised the president. She was a director of the Negro Affairs of the National Youth Administration.

j. He proposed a monthly pension of $200 for everyone over 60 years of age. The only requirement was that the person spend all of the money each month so that more money would be in circulation in the marketplace.

k. She was the first woman to fly across the Atlantic. She and her navigator began their around-the-world flight. The last messages from them were received when they were flying over the Pacific Ocean. Since then no trace of the plane has been found.

SUGGESTED TEACHING ACTIVITIES

1. Topics for further study:
   a. President F. D. Roosevelt
   b. Eleanor Roosevelt
   c. Tennessee Valley Authority
   d. Marian Anderson
   e. Huey P. Long
   f. Robert C. Weaver
   g. Father Coughlin
   h. Harold L. Ickes
   i. Harry Hopkins
   j. "court packing"
   k. Wagner Act
   l. Social Security Act
   m. William Hastie
   n. Mary McLeod Bethune
   o. Frances Perkins
   p. Francis E. Townsend
   q. John L. Lewis
   r. sit-down strike

2. Assign students to draw a political cartoon, using one of the following suggestions:
   a. Franklin Delano Roosevelt's victory in the presidential election of 1932
   b. The passage of the Social Security Act
   c. President Roosevelt's problems with the Supreme Court
   d. The passage of the Wagner Act

3. Assign students to study the provisions of the Social Security Act enacted in 1935. This act, more than any other, affected the lives of almost every American. What changes have been made in this act since 1935? Why? Why is the Social Security program becoming more and more expensive? What are the benefits of this act? The weaknesses? How does one get a Social Security number? Why should you have one? Interview family members or friends about how they feel about Social Security.

4. Read aloud selected excerpts from Terkel's *Hard Times* (New York: Pantheon Books, 1986) to students and discuss. Assign students to collect their own oral history by using a tape recorder in their interviews with people who lived during the 1930s. Describe life during that period. What did they think of President Roosevelt? Why? What do they remember about the "fireside chats"? How were their families able to provide food and shelter for themselves? Have students share the interviews with their classmates.

5. Assign students to prepare a chart showing how the Congress of Industrial Organization (CIO) and the American Federation of Labor (AFL) are similar and are different as to purpose, membership, leadership, and effectiveness.

6. Invite a guest to class who worked on one of the Civilian Conservation Corps projects to speak about his experiences in the camp and the kind of work that was accomplished.

7. Assign students to prepare a special written and/or oral report on the Tennessee Valley Authority (TVA). This project is considered one of the major achievements of the New Deal. Where was it located? Which states were included in this project? What was the purpose of developing this project? Did it accomplish its purpose? If you had been a member of Congress, would you have voted to pass legislation to develop the TVA? Why or why not? A bulletin board and/or dioramas can be made to show how the project was developed and how it affected the people living in the area.

8. Assign students to study an aspect of American culture during the 1930s. Some suggestions:
   a. recreation
   b. art and literature
   c. band leaders
   d. soap operas
   e. Jesse Owens
   f. radio programs
   g. comedians and singers
   h. magazines
   i. films and film stars

AMERICA FACES A GLOBAL CRISIS

When Franklin Delano Roosevelt became president in 1933, he tried to keep America away from global conflicts. By the late 1930s it appeared that the crises among foreign nations were becoming worse, threatening to create another war. The United States found it difficult to maintain its neutrality. By the fall of 1941, the United States was deeply involved in aiding the Allies. When the Japanese attacked Pearl Harbor on December 7, 1941, the Americans were ready to declare their active involvement in a global war.

The United States had participated in the Washington Conference of 1921 and the Kellogg-Briand Pact in 1928 in hopes of preventing a dangerous armaments race and reducing the possibility of war. The weak economy made it possible for powerful political leaders to take control, leaders who believed that the problems would be solved by expanding the nation's boundaries. Diplomacy in Europe was proving ineffective. Benito Mussolini's government in Italy was threatening to expand its borders. Adolf Hitler, leader of the Nazis in Germany, was becoming an aggressive power. In Asia, Japan was extending its control into Manchuria and China.

The United States was interested in increasing foreign trade. As Mussolini was preparing to invade Ethiopia to expand Italy's colonial holdings in Africa, the United States enacted the Neutrality Act of 1935. This act and the Neutrality Acts of 1936 and 1937 were designed to prevent events that had pressured the United States into entering World War I. The Neutrality Act of 1937 established the cash-and-carry policy. A nation could purchase only nonmilitary goods from the United States, and they had to pay cash and ship their purchases themselves.

Many events were changing the world. When General Francisco Franco revolted in July 1936 against the government in Spain, the United States did not offer assistance to either side. In the summer of 1937 Japan attacked China's five northern provinces. On December 12, 1937, the Japanese bombed and sank the U. S. gunboat, *Panay*, as it sailed the Yangtze River in China. In March 1938 German forces moved into Austria. Hitler demanded that Czechoslovakia give a part of the Sudetenland to Germany. Its people refused. Prime Minister Neville Chamberlain of Great Britain and others attending the meeting with Adolph Hitler on September 29 in Munich thought that the situation was peaceably resolved. However, in March 1939, Hitler occupied the remaining areas of Czechoslovakia and began threatening Poland. He claimed that the Poles had attacked the Germans. Hitler declared war on Poland. Great Britain and France then declared war on Germany. The global crisis had begun a second time.

President Roosevelt believed that armaments should be available to the Allied armies to help them offset the productive German munitions industry. The 1939 legislation prohibited American ships to enter the war zones. It did permit Allied ships to purchase arms on the same cash-and-carry basis that earlier Neutrality Acts had established for the sale of nonmilitary materials. The Soviets decided to take the Baltic republics. In the spring of 1940, Germany attacked Denmark and Norway and began its drive, with Italy, into France. Great Britain's new prime minister, Winston Churchill, requested ships and armaments from the Americans. President Roosevelt traded 50 American destroyers in return for the right to build American bases on British territory.

President Roosevelt decided to seek the presidency for the third term. He easily defeated his opponent, Wendell Willkie. The war was going badly and England could not meet the cash-and-carry requirements. Therefore, the United States lent or leased armaments to any nation who promised to return them when the war ended. Nazi forces invaded the Soviet Union. Lend-lease privileges were extended to the Russians. In October the German submarine sank the *Reuben James*, an American destroyer. Congress approved the arming of merchant vessels and allowed them to sail to nations at war. In August the Atlantic Charter outlined the war aims, the destruction of Nazism, and the principles upon which a better future for the world could be built.

The situation with Japan was deteriorating. Sunday morning, December 7, 1941, Japanese bombers attacked the naval base at Pearl Harbor. War was declared against Japan and three days later, Germany and Italy declared war on the United States. The Japanese inflicted heavy casualties on the United States. In Europe, Germany was bombarding the Soviet Union and Great Britain. The Allies agreed that the defeat of Germany would be first priority. Two broad offensives against the Japanese were planned after the fall of the Philippines. By the middle of 1943 the Japanese advances had finally been stopped.

When the American troops entered Germany, they liberated the concentration camps at which six million Jews were murdered by the Nazis. The mass murder became known as the Holocaust. Hitler and the Nazis had carried out a policy of ethnic destruction against the Jews.

The American economy was improving. Federal spending was putting more money in the marketplace. People were employed. Personal incomes, even those of the farmers, were increasing and consumer goods were in short supply. Wage earners put their earnings in savings which would, after the war, help keep the economic boom alive. The government was determined to prevent strikes and helped win important concessions for workers. The federal government was given authority to freeze agricultural prices, wages, salaries, and rents throughout the country. The sale of war bonds and increased taxes helped to finance the war. By the beginning of 1944, American factories were, in fact, producing more than the government needed.

The president of the Brotherhood of Sleeping Car Porters insisted that the government require companies receiving defense contracts to integrate the work forces. President Roosevelt promised to establish a Fair Employment Practices Commission. The purpose of this Commission was to investigate discrimination against Afro-Americans in war industries. Enforcement was limited but it was, at least, a step toward government commitment to racial equality. Afro-Americans migrated from rural areas of the South into industrial cities; jobs were available in munition plants. Sit-ins and demonstrations led by Afro-Americans aroused public awareness of racial discrimination. Young Afro-American men served bravely in the armed forces in spite of some discriminatory practices.

Many Native Americans also served in the military. For many, this was the first time they had left the reservations, some never to return. Some Native Americans served as "code-talkers," working in military communications and speaking their own languages over the radio and the telephones. The enemy would not know and understand the Native American dialect. Large numbers of

Mexican workers entered the work force to ease the labor shortage. Hispanic workers formed a large group of laborers in war plants. They encountered the same type of discrimination that Afro-Americans faced.

A major civil liberties violation occurred against the Japanese Americans during World War II. When Pearl Harbor was attacked, public hatred and intolerance toward Japanese Americans led to the circulation of stories about them being involved in plots and sabotage against the United States. None of the rumors were proved to be true. There were about 127,000 Japanese Americans living in a few concentrated areas in California. Two thirds of these people were naturalized or native-born American citizens (Nisei), and the others were first-generation immigrants (Issei). Under public pressure, in February 1942, the president authorized the army to intern the Japanese Americans. They were told to dispose of their property immediately and were taken to relocation centers to live until the end of the war. The Japanese Americans who resided in Hawaii were not relocated in centers. Not one Japanese American was ever convicted of disloyalty. The Japanese Americans in the armed forces established outstanding records for bravery and courage. The relocated Japanese Americans won compensation for their losses in the 1980s.

The New Deal was set aside for programs to "Win the War." By the end of 1943 the CCC and other programs such as the NYA and WPA were eliminated. President Roosevelt decided to run for the presidency a fourth time. He was suffering from serious health problems and was under great pressure. Senator Harry S Truman of Missouri was the vice presidential choice. The Democrats won.

German cities were being bombed by Allied forces. On the morning of June 6, 1944, a vast invasion force landed on the coast of Normandy, in France. In August the troops arrived in Paris and liberated France from German occupation. From there, the Allied troops advanced toward Germany. While the Allies were fighting their way through France, Soviet forces were sweeping westward into Central Europe and the Balkans. The German resistance was finally broken. On April 30 Hitler killed himself and on May 8, 1945, the remaining German forces surrendered unconditionally. The victory in Europe had come more quickly than expected. The victory in the Pacific was expected to take a little more time.

In the war against Japan, the United States fought at sea, on the islands in the Pacific, and on the mainland of Asia. The battles were long and difficult, and many soldiers lost their lives. Finally, General MacArthur's troops landed on Leyte Island in the Philippines. The defeat of Japan now seemed inevitable, but the war was not yet over. The marines took, from Japan, Iwo Jima and Okinawa with great American losses. In the meantime, President Roosevelt had died and Harry S Truman succeeded him as president.

Reports had reached the United States that Nazi scientists had learned to produce atomic fission in uranium. The United States and Great Britain immediately began to develop the weapon, hopefully, before the Germans did. On July 16, 1945, the Manhattan Project scientists witnessed the first atomic explosion in history. As soon as President Truman was notified of the atomic bomb while in Potsdam, he issued an ultimatum to the Japanese demanding that they surrender immediately. On August 3 President Truman ordered the use of the new atomic weapons against Japan when a settlement with Japan was not reached. There is controversy as to whether the United States was justified in using the bomb. On August 6, 1945, an atomic weapon was dropped on Hiroshima and then again on the city of Nagasaki, causing a great loss of life, horrendous wounds and illnesses to the civilians, and almost complete destruction of their cities. On September 2, 1945, on board the American battleship *Missouri*, Japanese officials surrendered.

The greatest war in the history of humankind came to an end. The United States now earned the title of superpower. The United States paid a high price for peace. In spite of the peace, the world continued to face an uncertain future as the United States and the U.S.S.R. (United Soviet Socialist Republic) emerged waging "a cold war."

THE THIRTY-SECOND PRESIDENT: FDR

Franklin Delano Roosevelt was one of the most popular presidents of the United States. He created government agencies, sometimes referred to as the alphabet soup, to cope with the problems of the Great Depression. As the conflict continued in Europe, he moved cautiously until the Japanese attacked Pearl Harbor. Then, under his leadership, the United States miraculously organized for war and fought the Japanese and helped the Allies with troops and supplies.

The following proclamation, the first official document issued by President Harry S Truman, expressed the feeling of Americans:

> **TO THE PEOPLE OF THE UNITED STATES:**
> It has pleased God in His infinite wisdom to take from us the immortal spirit of Franklin Delano Roosevelt, the thirty-second president of the United States.
>
> The leader of his people in a great war, he lived to see the assurance of the victory but not to share it. He lived to see the first foundations of the free and peaceful world to which his life was dedicated, but not to enter on that world himself.
>
> His fellow countrymen will sorely miss his fortitude and faith and courage in the time to come. The peoples of the earth who love the ways of freedom and of hope will mourn for him.
>
> But though his voice is silent, his courage is not spent, his faith is not extinguished. The courage of great men outlives them to become the courage of their people and the peoples of the world. It lives beyond them and upholds their purposes and brings their hopes to pass.

1. List three adjectives that you would use to describe President Roosevelt. Explain why you selected each one.

   _____

   _____

   _____

   _____

   _____

2. List what you think are five major achievements of President Roosevelt, when each was accomplished, and how it promoted a better way of life for people and peace for the world.

   _____

   _____

   _____

   _____

   _____

WHICH EVENT HAPPENED FIRST?

Place the letter of the event that happened first in the blank at the left.

_____1.   a. Munich Conference is held to discuss Adolf Hitler's demands in Czechoslovakia.
            b. Adolf Hitler becomes Chancellor of Germany.

_____2.   a. The Japanese attack Pearl Harbor on a Sunday morning in December.
            b. Italy, under the leadership of Benito Mussolini, invades Ethiopia.

_____3.   a. Franklin Delano Roosevelt is elected president of the United States.
            b. Germany invades Czechoslovakia and Poland.

_____4.   a. Japanese Americans are interned in relocation centers.
            b. The Atlantic Charter is signed by President Roosevelt and Prime Minister
               Winston Churchill.

_____5.   a. President Franklin Delano Roosevelt is reelected president for the first time.
            b. The United States drops the atomic bomb on Hiroshima.

_____6.   a. The Allied forces invade Normandy.
            b. Japan officially surrenders to the United States.

_____7.   a. President Roosevelt is reelected president for the last time.
            b. President Roosevelt proclaims the Good Neighbor Policy with the Latin American
               nations.

_____8.   a. The Manhattan Projects begin their work in the United States.
            b. Marian Anderson sings at the Lincoln Memorial instead of the DAR auditorium.

_____9.   a. The Congress of Industrial Organizations is established with John L. Lewis as its
               first president.
            b. The American forces recapture the Philippines.
            c. The Soviet Union invades the Baltic nations and Finland.

_____10.   a. American forces capture Okinawa.
            b. Germany surrenders to the Allied Forces.
            c. Japan invades Manchuria.

_____11.   a. The Washington Conference leads to reductions in naval armaments.
            b. Japan attacks the U. S. gunboat, *Panay*.
            c. Germany surrenders to the Allies.

_____12.   a. President Roosevelt dies and Harry S Truman becomes president of the United
               States.
            b. The Japanese Americans are interned in relocation centers.
            c. President Roosevelt establishes the Fair Employment Practices Commission.

SUGGESTED TEACHING ACTIVITIES

1. Suggested topics for further study:
   a. Good Neighbor Policy
   b. Benito Mussolini
   c. Neutrality Acts
   d. gunboat, *Panay*
   e. *Lebensraum*
   f. Adolf Hitler
   g. atrocities
   h. Holocaust
   i. Neville Chamberlain
   j. Winston Churchill
   k. Munich Conference
   l. Franklin Delano Roosevelt
   m. Pearl Harbor
   n. destroyer, *Reuben James*
   o. General MacArthur
   p. George C. Marshall
   q. Japanese Americans
   r. General Eisenhower
   s. General Stilwell
   t. General Rommel
   u. Burma or Ledo Road
   v. Manhattan Project
   w. Fair Employment Practice Commission

2. The atomic bomb was dropped over Hiroshima, destroying the city and killing thousands of people. Still, the Japanese would not surrender. A few days later a second bomb was dropped on Nagasaki. President Harry S Truman made the decision, believing that he had no choice but to use the atomic bomb. He justified his decision by saying, "We have used it (bomb) against those who attacked us without warning at Pearl Harbor, against those who have starved and beaten and executed American prisoners of war, against those who have abandoned all pretense of obeying international laws of warfare. We have used it in order to shorten the agony of war, in order to save the lives of thousands and thousands of young Americans." Assign students to write a composition stating how they feel about the use of atomic weapons in war. Did they feel that President Truman was justified? Why? If they had been President Truman, would they have made the same decision? Why or why not?

3. Read orally to the class Toshi Maruki's book entitled *Hiroshima No Pika* (New York: Lothrop, Lee & Shepard Books, 1980). This is a powerful and highly emotional statement about war. Class Discussion: What is the meaning of war? What are the consequences of war? What are the responsibilities of human beings toward other human beings?

4. Read orally to the class Roberto Innocenti's book entitled *Rose Blanche* (Mankato, Minnesota: Creative Education Inc., 1985). This, too, is a powerful statement about war and peace. Class Discussion: Do children understand what war is? What was the Holocaust? How does this book make you feel about war? About peace?

5. Student Assignment: Prepare a chart listing at least six important sea and/or land battles fought during World War II, date, location, importance, parties involved, and the outcome's effect on the war. Then, locate the sites of these battles on an outline map of the world.

6. Assign students to prepare a short written report on one of the generals who fought during World War II. What qualities of leadership did this individual possess? How did he demonstrate his talents as a military leader? Tell something about his early life, family, and career.

7. Assign student volunteers to prepare a display of posters which were used during World War II to recruit young men for military service, to sell bonds, and to work in war plants. Also, they might prepare a list of songs that were popular during World War II and film stars who performed for servicemen overseas.

8. Invite a World War II veteran and/or army nurse to speak to the class about their experiences during the war in the Pacific or European theater or assign students to interview with a tape recorder a veteran and/or nurse of World War II and to share the tapes with their classmates.

THE COLD WAR

After the defeat of Germany and Japan, the United States began a struggle, referred to as the cold war, with the Soviet Union. It developed slowly, with minor differences involving conflicts without military action in economic and foreign policies. Some of the situations, though, almost threatened war. People in the United States, during the middle 1940s, were enjoying prosperity and a high standard of living. At the same time, they were frightened that the cold war would bring about a "hot" war.

There were fundamental differences between the Soviet Union and the United States as to what the world should be like after World War II. The Americans were suspicious of the Russians and they, in turn, were suspicious of the Americans. During the war, the leaders of the Allies met to discuss military strategies and plans for the postwar world. Roosevelt, Churchill, and Joseph Stalin met together for the first time in Teheran, Iran, and planned military strategy against the Germans and agreed to establish an international organization to keep peace. The Dumbarton Oaks Conference was scheduled in 1944 to draw up more specific plans for the United Nations.

The three leaders met again in the Soviet city of Yalta, in 1945, to discuss the approaching end of hostilities and the fate of Poland. Roosevelt and Churchill wanted a government in Poland which would cooperate with Western European nations, and Stalin insisted that the Polish needed a Communist government. Unfortunately, President Roosevelt suffered a sudden stroke and died in 1945, and Harry S Truman succeeded him as president. President Truman found himself facing difficult global problems.

After the war, Soviet troops remained in Poland. Disagreement existed among the allied powers about the future of Germany. Finally, Germany was divided into four zones controlled by the United States, France, Great Britain, and the Soviet Union. Berlin, which was located in the Soviet zone, was also divided into four zones. Great Britain, France, and the United States decided to join their zones into one nation. This angered the Soviets who were afraid that Germany might become a powerful nation again. In 1948 the Soviets tried to force the other nations out of Berlin by blockading the city. No one could get in or out of Berlin. The Allies organized a successful airlift to get food and supplies to Berliners. The Soviets finally lifted the blockade in 1949. Hungary, Yugoslavia, Albania, Bulgaria, and Romania were under Soviet control by 1947. These nations, with Poland, were known as the "iron curtain countries."

In Asia a civil war was being fought in China. The Nationalist government, under the leadership of Chiang Kai-shek, was fighting the Communists, led by Mao Zedong. The United States supported Chiang Kai-shek because they feared the spread of communism in Asia. Mao Zedong was successful in driving Chiang Kai-shek's forces to Taiwan, an island off the coast of China. China was now under Communist control.

America's new policy was to "contain" the threat of any Soviet expansion. When the Soviets threatened Turkey and Greece, President Truman, in a speech before Congress in 1947, presented the "Truman Doctrine" which promised assistance to people to develop their own countries in their own way. Congress immediately approved military aid and economic assistance to Greece. In 1948 Secretary of State George C. Marshall announced a plan, the Marshall Plan, which offered American financial assistance in rebuilding the economies of European countries.

To resist the aggressive actions of the Soviet Union, Western European nations and the United States signed an agreement in 1949 establishing the North Atlantic Treaty Organization (NATO). An armed attack against one member of the organization would be considered an attack against all. The Soviet Union created the Warsaw Pact, in 1955, with the Communist governments of Eastern Europe.

When the Soviet Union announced the explosion of its first atomic weapon and Chiang Kai-shek's government fled to Taiwan, President Truman decided to review American foreign policy. The National Security Council report recommended that the United States expand its military power and assume the responsibility of defending freedom in the world.

Even as government spending dropped after the war, the demand for consumer goods increased. The GI Bill of Rights (1944) provided economic and educational assistance to returning veterans. Prices increased rapidly for all kinds of consumer goods. The workers demanded pay raises, and labor disputes were common in many industries. The United Mine workers went on strike, closing down the coal fields for over a month. President Truman ordered the men back to work and forced the mine owners to meet most of the union's demands. The president also pressured the railroad workers to return to their jobs after striking. The Taft-Hartley Act of 1947 was passed by Congress over President Truman's veto. This act created more restrictions on unions by introducing new procedures for collective bargaining. The closed shop was now illegal. This meant that someone could be hired without being a member of a union.

A few days after the surrender of Japan, President Truman presented to Congress a domestic program called the "Fair Deal." This expanded Social Security benefits, formed a permanent Fair Employment Practices Act, provided public housing and slum clearance, and many other programs. Later, he added federal aid to education and a plan for health insurance. The "Fair Deal" made little progress in Congress. Most of the programs were defeated.

During the Convention of 1948, the Democrats reluctantly gave the presidential nomination to Harry S Truman. The Republicans nominated Governor Thomas E. Dewey of New York. Many people thought that President Truman's bid for the presidency was hopeless. Nevertheless, he campaigned tirelessly. "I'm going to fight hard. I'm going to give them hell!" He let the people know how he felt about the "do nothing good for nothing Republican Congress." He wanted a repeal of the Taft-Hartley Act, increased price supports for farmers, and strong civil rights protection for African Americans. It was one of the most dramatic upsets in the history of presidential elections when Harry S Truman won.

After the election, President Truman continued to have problems with Congress. He did, though, win three important issues. Congress raised the legal minimum wage. It approved an expansion of the Social Security System, and it strengthened the government's commitment to federal housing. He continued to work for civil rights.

In 1950 the North Korean Communist armies invaded South Korea. Americans found themselves involved in a "limited war." At the end of World War II, neither the United States nor the Soviet Union were willing to withdraw their troops from Korea. Because of this situation, Korea had been divided, temporarily, along the parallel. The Soviets left after making certain that North Korea had a strong Communist government, supported by a strong army. The Americans left South Korea a few months later.

President Truman ordered American forces to help the South Koreans to protect themselves against the invaders. On the same day, he asked the United Nations to intervene. The United Nations agreed to call for international assistance for Syngman Rhee's government in South Korea. General Douglas MacArthur served as commander of the United Nations operations. The troops were mostly Americans.

The U. N. forces were advancing until they realized that North Koreans were receiving assistance from the Chinese. The U. N. forces were pushed back until the South Korean capital of Seoul was captured. Again, the United Nations advanced, regaining what they had lost. President Truman did not want a war with China, and he was trying to negotiate a solution to the conflict. General MacArthur was critical of the president's policy and wanted to confront the Chinese militarily. President Truman, on April 11, 1951, dismissed General MacArthur from his command. Prominent military leaders supported President Truman's decision. The "limited war" continued until 1958. Americans had won a great victory in World War II, but now they were unable to stop North Korea's advances. Some people felt something was wrong in the United States; people were fearful of communism and uneasy within their own country.

The Republicans attacked the Democrats, maintaining that they allowed Communists to gain power and to undermine the American government. Many Hollywood film stars, producers, and writers were accused of sympathizing with the Communists. The House Un-American Activities Committee accused reputable members of the State Department of espionage, or spying.

Fear increased, too, when, in 1947, President Truman issued an executive order which provided for the establishment of loyalty boards to examine the personal and political activities of federal employees. Those persons who were proven to be disloyal or who were thought to be security risks were expected to be fired. The McCarran Internal Security Act was passed in 1950. It required all Communist organizations to register with the government and to publish their records. It prohibited aliens suspected of Communist contacts to enter the United States, and it allowed those already here to be deported. The Federal Bureau of Investigation and the Justice Department investigated and tried to convict people involved in Communist conspiracies to steal America's atomic secrets for the Soviet Union. Julius Rosenberg and his wife Ethel, members of the Communist party, were accused of giving atomic secrets to the Soviet Union. They denied their guilt. Nevertheless, they were convicted of spying and sentenced to death in the electric chair.

National security was a major issue after the war. Joseph McCarthy, a Republican senator from Wisconsin, conducted investigations to check Communist activities in the United States. These investigations were highly publicized. He often used false evidence and terrorized many people, most of them innocent. In December 1954, the Senate finally censured Senator McCarthy.

During the 1952 Democratic presidential convention, Governor Adlai E. Stevenson of Illinois was nominated for president, and the Republicans nominated General Dwight D. Eisenhower for the presidency and Richard Nixon for the vice presidency. General Eisenhower pledged to go to Korea, if necessary, to end the "limited war." General Eisenhower won both the popular and the electoral vote by a landslide. Twenty years of Democratic rule came to an end.

PRESIDENTIAL ELECTIONS

Study the following chart:

YEAR	CANDIDATES	PARTIES	POPULAR VOTE	ELECTORAL VOTE
1944	Franklin D. Roosevelt	Democratic	25,602,504	432
	Thomas E. Dewey	Republican	22,006,285	99
1948	Harry S Truman	Democratic	24,105,695	304
	Thomas E. Dewey	Republican	21,969,170	189
	J. Strom Thurmond	State-Rights Democratic	1,169,021	38
	Henry A. Wallace	Progressive	1,156,103	0
1952	Dwight D. Eisenhower	Republican	33,936,252	442
	Adlai E. Stevenson	Democratic	27,314,992	89

1. Harry S Truman won the 1948 presidential election. Why do you think everyone was surprised?

_____

_____

_____

2. List at least five ideas you have learned about presidential elections from studying this chart.

_____

_____

_____

_____

_____

3. Which candidate would you have voted for in 1948? Why? (List at least three reasons.)

_____

_____

_____

4. Which candidate would you have voted for in 1952? Why? (List at least three reasons.)

_____

_____

_____

MAKING CONNECTIONS WITH TERMS AND MEANINGS

Connect the terms in Column I with their definitions in Column II.

COLUMN I

_____1. GI Bill of Rights

_____2. containment policy

_____3. "iron curtain"

_____4. Berlin airlift

_____5. Marshall Plan

_____6. Truman Doctrine

_____7. "limited war"

_____8. treaty

_____9. subversive

_____10. censure

_____11. cold war

_____12. reparations

_____13. espionage

_____14. treason

COLUMN II

a. A formal agreement completed between two or more countries concerning peace, mutual protection, or trade.

b. The betrayal of one's country by aiding or joining the enemy.

c. When the Soviets blockaded the capital of Germany, the Allies organized an airlift to get food and other supplies to the city.

d. An organization or an individual who intends to destroy or overthrow the government in power.

e. Compensations paid by a defeated country or countries to the victorious nation or nations for war damages.

f. Legislation which was passed after World War II which provided veterans with benefits in education, housing, employment, and health.

g. To scold or reprimand someone officially for his/her behavior.

h. This involves the use of spies to collect information about the activities and plans of another nation.

i. The offer of U. S. aid to needy European nations to erase hunger and poverty and to improve the economy.

j. This policy suggested that the United States would become involved in aiding countries in their struggles against totalitarian governments and communism.

k. The existence of political and/or economic conflicts between nations, yet no military action is taken.

l. This policy tries to prevent the spread of an opposing nation's influence.

m. Warfare waged between two or more nations in which each side limits military involvement.

n. A term first used by Prime Minister Churchill to describe the line between Soviet-controlled Eastern European nations and the Western European nations.

SUGGESTED TEACHING ACTIVITIES

1. Topics for further study:
   a. Truman Doctrine
   b. Joseph Stalin
   c. Dumbarton Oaks Conference
   d. Thomas E. Dewey
   e. Fair Deal
   f. Adlai Stevenson
   g. Joseph McCarthy
   h. Marshall Plan
   i. containment policy
   j. Winston Churchill
   k. Teheran Conference
   l. Alger Hiss
   m. Julius and Ethel Rosenberg
   n. General Douglas MacArthur
   o. Poland
   p. iron curtain countries
   q. Dwight D. Eisenhower
   r. Chiang Kai-shek
   s. Taiwan
   t. NATO
   u. GI Bill of Rights
   v. Richard Nixon
   w. Korea
   x. Berlin airlift
   y. China
   z. Mao Zedong

2. Assign students to locate the following places on a map of Asia which includes China, Korea, and Japan: North Korea, South Korea, Pyongyang, Seoul, Pusan, Inchon, Panmunjom, China, Japan, Taiwan, Yellow Sea, and Korean Strait. How was the United States involved in this area of the world? Why? What role did the United States assume when North Korea invaded South Korea? Why? Why was there criticism of the "limited war" fought in Korea?

3. The charter of the United Nations was officially adopted by the delegates from 46 nations at the San Francisco Conference. Assign students to study any one of the many problems confronting the United Nations and write a short composition explaining how it was handled (for example; the conflicting claims of the Jews and Arabs to Palestine or participating in the Korean conflict).

4. In the presidential election of 1948, the Democrats nominated Harry S Truman, and the Republicans selected Thomas E. Dewey as their candidate. No one thought the Democrats would win this election since President Truman was so unpopular. Also, the Democrats had been in power too long and people wanted a change. The Republicans were certain of a victory. On the chalkboard, have the students list the reasons why they think Harry S Truman won the election. Some students may volunteer to bring in copies of the first page of newspapers announcing his victory.

5. Assign students to write a short biographical report of Eleanor Roosevelt, Harry S Truman, General Douglas MacArthur, General George C. Marshall, Joseph McCarthy, Joseph Stalin, or Winston Churchill. What influence did each of these individuals have in politics and in the betterment of life in his/her own country and in the world? Is his/her influence still felt in today's world? Explain.

6. Assign students to interview veterans of World War II or the Korean War and to share their findings with classmates. Questions should be prepared before the actual interview takes place. What did the veterans think of war? Their generals? The president of the United States? The purpose of the war? Did any of them receive benefits from the GI Bill? How did it help them and their families?

7. Prepare a time line for the classroom to include the following events: Atlantic Charter drafted, Teheran Conference, passage of GI Bill of Rights, Yalta Conference, death of President F. D. Roosevelt, United Nations founded, Truman Doctrine announced, Marshall Plan proposed, Berlin airlift, Truman's election to the presidency, NATO established, beginning of the Korean War, dismissal of General MacArthur, Dwight D. Eisenhower elected president.

8. Assign students to draw political cartoons depicting an issue during the cold war period such as the election of President Harry S Truman or the Berlin airlift. Display the cartoons in the classroom.

PROSPERITY AND THE AMERICAN SOCIETY

During the 1950s and early 1960s the Americans had achieved the highest standard of living of any society in the history of the world. Economic growth, with its booming prosperity, brought about many changes in American life. Nevertheless, there were serious problems within the American society. The struggle with the Soviets in the cold war continued. The prosperity was not shared with everyone. In 1950 about 30 million people lived in poverty. Minorities continued to suffer discriminatory practices socially, politically, and economically.

Government spending continued to stimulate growth. Increased public funding of housing, schools, and highways contributed to the prosperity. The Korean War, demanding military weapons and planes, boosted the economy. The productivity of workers increased as new production techniques and mechanical efficiency were developed. Electronic computers made business more efficient and also increased the demand for highly trained experts, such as engineers and scientists. The national population began to increase after the war. In 1950 there were 150 million people living in the United States. In 1960 that number increased to 179 million. People were also moving into the suburbs, demanding more housing and automobiles as well the construction of more roads.

People thought that government should regulate the economy without interfering directly with private businesses. A British economist, John Maynard Keynes, believed that regulation of government spending and the amount of money in the marketplace would determine the state of the economy. According to this idea, government should be able to stimulate the economy to avoid a depression. Americans also assumed that there would be economic growth permanently. If production continued, the poorest families would be able to raise their quality of living.

During the 1950s a few large corporations controlled the nation's economy. With increased mechanization, the need for farm labor was reduced. New fertilizers and improved irrigation techniques helped to increase agricultural productivity. The family farm was disappearing and corporations and very wealthy landowners controlled the agricultural production of the country. The labor organizations became more powerful during this period of time. In 1948 Walter Reuther, president of the United Automobile Workers, received many benefits and gains for automobile workers. Non-union workers, though, in small factories did not receive the benefits earned by union workers. The American Federation of Labor and the Congress of Industrial Organizations merged to create the AFL-CIO in 1955.

Advertisements appeared nationally on radio, television, and billboards for consumer goods—radios, televisions, dishwashers, and automobiles. Sometimes credit cards were used to make these purchases. After the war, people wanted to be with their families; they wanted privacy, security, and space. Innovations in housing construction and the movement of families to the suburbs brought a boom to the construction market.

After the war, television became the most powerful medium of mass communication in history. In spite of the criticism regarding television and television programming, it was and continues to be important in shaping social values and political ideas. Most of the entertainment programs reflected the values of middle-class Americans. Those people who were not representative of the middle class often developed a sense of alienation or separateness and hopelessness because of their exclusion from the "television world." The critics during this period were known as the "beats" or the "beatniks." They disliked the American middle-class society and they felt it should be avoided. To them, it was too conforming and meaningless. Small farmers were doing poorly as were people living in the city ghettos, Appalachian regions, and other poverty areas. These areas were known as "the other America"—an America of poverty and hopelessness.

Americans were fascinated with science and space. Many new drugs and treatments were discovered to help the sick. Jonas Salk discovered a vaccine to prevent polio. There was a decline in infant mortality, and the life expectancy age rose to 71. The space program was very popular. After the Soviets launched *Sputnik* into space, Americans demanded improvement in the teaching of science and mathematics in schools. The National Defense Education Act of 1958 provided federal funding for the development of teaching programs in science, mathematics, and foreign languages. Also, more research laboratories were established and the space exploration program was developed. Astronauts Alan Shepard and John Glenn became American heroes. Neil Armstrong and Edwin Aldrin, Jr., achieved fame when they walked on the moon.

The struggle for civil rights began in 1954 with a Supreme Court decision. In the case of *Brown v. Board of Education of Topeka, Kansas,* the Court rejected the 1896 decision that permitted public schools to be separated by race, or *segregated.* Segregated schools were now illegal. All public schools had to be for all Americans, and they had to be integrated. Chief Justice Earl Warren, appointed to the Court by President Eisenhower, stated, "We conclude that in the field of public education the doctrine of 'separate but equal' has no place. Separated educational facilities are inherently unequal." In September 1957 in Little Rock, Arkansas, several Afro-American students were denied entry into Central High School. Governor Orval Faubus ordered the National Guard to intervene to stop the integration of the city's Central High School. The governor finally called off the National Guard, and President Eisenhower responded by sending federal troops to Little Rock to restore order and ensure that the court orders would be obeyed.

The Brown decision helped to stimulate other challenges to segregation. Rosa Parks, an Afro-American woman, was arrested when she refused to give up her seat on a Montgomery bus to a white passenger. She was not the first to defy the law, but she was able to represent the thousands of hard-working Americans who deserved better. Once started, this boycott was very effective. The buses in Montgomery abandoned their discriminatory seating policies, and the boycott came to an end. The leader of the boycott movement was Martin Luther King, Jr., son of a prominent Atlanta minister. His approach was based on the doctrine of nonviolence or passive resistance. He urged Afro-Americans to participate in peaceful demonstrations, to allow themselves to be arrested, even beaten, if necessary. His followers responded to hate with love. Reverend Martin Luther King, Jr., became an influential and widely admired leader working for civil rights. Unfortunately, he was assassinated in 1968. His approach to the problems of segregation led the Brooklyn Dodgers to sign Jackie Robinson to play for them. By the middle of the 1950s Afro-Americans were hired to play in professional sports and the armed forces were integrated.

President Eisenhower was a popular president who was conservative in his thinking and pursued a moderate course in his policies. His cabinet was described as including eight millionaires and a plumber, Secretary of Labor Martin P. Durkin. He delegated authority to his staff, and he tended to support private rather than public development of natural resources. His goal was to limit governmental involvement in the economy. He lowered federal support for farm prices, removed wage and price controls, and opposed social service programs and health care insurance. In fact, President Eisenhower ended his term with $1 billion surplus. He was responsible for extending social security and building highways while he was in office.

President Eisenhower's first item of business when he became president was to end the war in Korea. An agreement was signed on July 27, 1953, after months of negotiations, ending the war and dividing North and South Korea at the thirty-eighth parallel. President Eisenhower appointed John Foster Dulles, a corporate lawyer who fought communism with diplomacy, as his Secretary of State. He integrated non-Communist countries in a system of mutual defense pacts such as SEATO and CENTO.

In Southeast Asia, the United States was being drawn into another conflict. France wanted to restore its authority over Vietnam, its former colony. In 1954 French troops became surrounded in a siege of the city of Dienbienphu, which they were incapable of defending. They suffered defeat, surrendered, and left the country. The United States intervened to prevent the total collapse of the French military effort. A pro-American government was established in South Vietnam, headed by Ngo Dinh Diem, a wealthy member of the country's Roman Catholic minority. The United States government provided military advisers and equipment to help South Vietnam, for fear that it might become Communist.

The Middle East was another area demanding attention. After World War II, the United Nations divided the land of Palestine between the Palestinian Arabs and the Jews. The new homeland of the Jews, Israel, was recognized by the United States and the Soviet Union. The establishment of a Jewish state in Palestine was the beginning of the battle for a homeland. Palestinian Arabs, unwilling to accept being displaced in their own country in 1948, fought one of several Arab-Israeli wars. The area had the richest oil reserves in the world. Both the American economy and the world economy depended on the Middle East for oil. Premier Mohammad Mossadegh, leader of Iran, tried to nationalize the British-controlled oil industry. He was replaced with Mohammad Reza Phalavi, who became the Shah of Iran. The Shah of Iran allowed American companies to share in the development of Iranian oil reserves. In 1956 Gamal Abdel Nasser, leader of the Egyptian government, seized control of the Suez Canal from Great Britain.

In Latin America, the Cubans revolted in 1959 and overthrew Fulgencio Batista and his government. A new government was formed by Fidel Castro who promised many reforms. He banned opposition parties and refused to hold elections. He publicly declared that he was a Communist. In 1960 he signed a trade agreement with the Soviet Union, and the United States refused to buy Cuban sugar. The United States' relationship with Cuba deteriorated.

The arms race continued to be a serious problem. Not only were the tensions increased between the United States and the Soviets, but tensions existed with other nations, too. A meeting was planned in 1960 between Premier Khrushchev and President Eisenhower in Paris. Shortly after the meeting, President Eisenhower would visit the Soviet Union. Before the scheduled meeting in Paris, the Soviets announced that they had shot down an American U-2 high altitude spy plane over Soviet territory and that its pilot, Francis Gary Powers, was captured. The summit meeting did not take place, and Premier Khrushchev withdrew his invitation inviting President Eisenhower to Moscow.

LABOR FORCE

Study the following chart:

Year	% IN LABOR FORCE Farm Occupation	Nonfarm Occupation	Year	% IN LABOR FORCE Farm Occupation	Nonfarm Occupation
1840	68.6	31.4	1920	27.0	73.0
1850	63.7	36.3	1930	21.4	78.6
1860	58.9	41.1	1940	17.4	82.6
1870	53.0	47.0	1950	11.6	88.4
1880	49.4	50.6	1960	6.0	94.0
1890	42.6	57.4	1970	3.1	96.9
1900	37.5	62.5	1980	2.2	97.8
1910	31.0	69.0	1990	1.6	98.4

1. What are five things that you have learned about the labor force as you studied this chart?

_____

_____

_____

_____

_____

2. Why do you think there was such a great drop of labor in farm occupations after 1960?

_____

_____

3. In which year were there more people working in nonfarm occupations than in farm occupations? Can you think of any reasons why this happened?

_____

_____

_____

4. What do you think the percentages will be in the year 2000? Why?

_____

_____

"IFFY" QUESTIONS

Respond to any two of the following questions. For each question list and explain the reasons for your action.

1. If you had been President Eisenhower, would you have sent federal troops to Little Rock, Arkansas?
2. If you were serving in the United States Congress during the 1950s, would you have approved sending military advisers and equipment to Vietnam?
3. If you had been a member of the United Nations, would you have voted to divide the land of Palestine between the Palestinian Arabs and the Jews to create Israel?
4. If you had lived in Montgomery, Alabama, during the bus boycott, would you have participated in this boycott?

_____

_____

_____

_____

_____

_____

_____

_____

_____

_____

_____

_____

_____

_____

_____

_____

_____

_____

_____

_____

_____

SUGGESTED TEACHING ACTIVITIES

1. Topics for further study:
   a. John Maynard Keynes
   b. Walter Reuther
   c. Neil Armstrong
   d. beatniks
   e. astronauts
   f. John Glenn
   g. Gamal Abdel Nasser
   h. Dag Hammarskjöld
   i. Rosa Parks
   j. Jonas Salk
   k. Rev. Martin Luther King, Jr.
   l. Charles E. Wilson
   m. Jackie Robinson
   n. Shah of Iran
   o. Chief Justice Earl Warren
   p. John Foster Dulles
   q. *Sputnik*
   r. Alan Shepard
   s. Israel
   t. Premier Nikita Khrushchev
   u. J. Robert Oppenheimer
   v. Fidel Castro
   w. Vietnam
   x. television

2. Assign students to imagine that they are Afro-American students who wanted to enroll in Central High School, Little Rock, Arkansas. Have them write entries into a diary and/or journal for five days telling how they felt when they saw the federal troops, parents, and other students on registration day. Then, tell how they were treated by students and teachers as they attended their classes.

3. Dag Hammarskjöld served as secretary general of the United Nations from 1953 until 1961 when he was killed in a plane crash. He believed strongly in the goals and purposes of the United Nations and demonstrated patience, courage, and insightfulness as he helped the members reach an understanding of all sides of issues which were debated in the assembly. Assign students to write a short composition telling about the personal and professional qualities of Dag Hammarskjöld which made him an outstanding leader. How is one selected to serve as secretary general? Also, assign students to prepare a list of all the persons who served as secretary general of the United Nations, noting when and for how long.

4. Reverend Martin Luther King, Jr., was asked to lead the Montgomery bus boycott in 1955 when Rosa Parks refused to give up her seat to a white passenger on the bus. Assign students to read about him or to interview people who were acquainted with his work. Class discussion: How did Reverend King, Jr., improve the conditions of Afro-Americans? What personal qualities made him a great leader? How was he influenced by Mahatma Ghandi? Why did he receive the Nobel Peace Prize?

5. Assign student volunteers to write a television script enacting the episodes involved in the Montgomery bus boycott in Alabama. If possible, prepare a videotape of the script and share the creative production with classmates.

6. Assign students to prepare a time line which includes the following events:
   a. Alan Shepard becomes the first American in space.
   b. Jackie Robinson is signed to play in major leagues.
   c. Premier Joseph Stalin dies.
   d. Supreme Court rules on *Brown v. Board of Education*.
   e. Americans land on the moon.
   f. Eisenhower is reelected president.
   g. Nikita Khrushchev visits the U. S.
   h. Soviet Union launches *Sputnik*.
   i. Suez crisis occurs.
   j. AFL and CIO merge.
   k. Korean War ends.
   l. Montgomery bus boycott takes place.

HOPES AND FRUSTRATIONS OF THE SIXTIES

The sixties were difficult years as the United States became involved in serious social problems as well as in cultural and political crises. The Democratic Convention in 1959 nominated John Fitzgerald Kennedy as the presidential candidate and Lyndon B. Johnson as the vice presidential candidate. The Democrats won by one of the narrowest victories in the history of presidential elections.

In his inaugural address, President Kennedy appeared to direct his comments to young people. "Let the word go forth from this time and place, to friend and foe alike, that the torch has been passed to a new generation of Americans. My fellow Americans, ask not what your country can do for you—ask what you can do for your country." He believed in an active government, and his idea of presidential leadership was noticeable in foreign policy and in his own personal style. His "New Frontier" program proposed many reforms, but he was unable to gain support for them in Congress. He was able, though, to increase international trade and to stabilize the economy. During his administration, he established the Peace Corps overseas as well as expanded the American commitment to volunteer work in the United States. While he and the first lady were being driven in an open car in Dallas, Texas, he was assassinated on November 23, 1963. Americans were shocked and bewildered. President Kennedy had been a symbol of hope for many people.

Lyndon B. Johnson became the thirty-sixth president of the United States. He was different from President Kennedy. President Johnson was able to manage Congress and succeeded in getting some of the New Frontier proposals passed. President Johnson also proposed a reform program of his own, the "Great Society." He won approval of much of that program by using his management and persuasive skills. In the next presidential election, President Johnson received more votes than any candidate before him.

President Kennedy and President Johnson shared two basic goals. They both worked toward maintaining a stable and prosperous economy and expanding the responsibilities of the federal government for the general social welfare. Kennedy revised the minimum wage law, extended coverage to more workers, and raised the minimum hourly wage. Another important program enacted in 1965 was Medicare, which provided federal aid to the elderly for medical expenses. When President Johnson assumed the presidency, he began "an unconditional war on poverty." In 1966 he pressured the passage of the Medicaid program which extended federal medical assistance to welfare recipients of all ages. He established the Office of Economic Opportunity which created programs such as Head Start and job training for the poor. Community Action programs encouraged people to develop their skills and seek more training. These programs helped to reduce poverty in certain areas, but did not eliminate poverty altogether. President Johnson established the Department of Housing and Urban Development and the Model Cities program to help decrease problems of poverty in urban areas.

The Elementary and Secondary Education Act of 1965 extended federal funding to education. President Johnson tried to deal with social issues such as poverty, health care, education, the environment, consumer protection, agriculture, and many others. The Immigration Act of 1965 continued to limit immigration from some parts of Latin America, but it permitted people from all parts of Europe, Asia, and Africa to enter the United States on an equal basis. These reforms cost money which helped to increase federal spending.

The battle for racial equality could not be ignored. In 1960 Afro-American students in North Carolina staged a sit-in at a Woolworth's lunch counter. Many similar demonstrations occurred elsewhere, forcing many businesses to integrate their facilities. In 1960 the Student Nonviolent Coordinating Committee was formed. In 1961 the Congress of Racial Equality began the "freedom rides" to force desegregation of bus and train stations. In October 1962, a federal court ordered the University of Mississippi to enroll James Meredith as a student. President Kennedy sent federal troops to protect Meredith's right to attend the university. Many other demonstrations were taking place which were reported on television.

President Kennedy confronted the issue of race and introduced legislative proposals to prohibit segregation in public accommodations and discrimination in employment. He also increased the power of the government to file suits on behalf of school integration. Opposition in Congress was great. In August 1963, Afro-Americans marched to the Lincoln Memorial for a civil rights demonstration. There, Martin Luther King, Jr., gave his memorable speech, "I have a dream." In March 1965, Martin Luther King, Jr., helped to organize a major demonstration by Afro-Americans in Selma, Alabama, demanding the right to register to vote. The confrontation between the peaceful demonstrators and the sheriff of Selma led to a brutal attack on the demonstrators. President Johnson was able to win the passage of the Civil Rights Act of 1965 which provided federal protection to Afro-Americans attempting to exercise their right to vote.

Now, the struggle shifted to the demands of poor urban Afro-Americans. The living conditions of Afro-Americans in the cities were deplorable. These people were victims of crime and drug addiction, living in substandard housing. Johnson gave support to the concept of "affirmative action" for past injustices in 1965. Quota systems and job "preferences" were used to bring about affirmative action. Civil rights activists were directing their attention to housing and employment discrimination. Urban poverty was a serious problem. Riots in cities, such as New York City, Los Angeles (Watts), Chicago, Detroit, and Cleveland were devastating.

Now, Afro-Americans were turning to black power. Black power could mean many things. It was a belief in the importance of Afro-American self-reliance. Other organizations began to emerge outside the established civil rights movement such as the Black Panthers and the Nation of Islam. These groups worked for complete racial separation. Malcolm X, a leader of the militant Black Muslims, was assassinated during a meeting. He continues to be honored and revered by many Afro-Americans.

The Kennedy and Johnson administrations dealt with problems in foreign policy as they did with domestic ones. They used a positive and active approach. However, as in domestic problems, their approach overseas brought both benefits and disasters. President Kennedy insisted on increases in the nation's nuclear armaments and supported the training of soldiers to fight modern, limited wars. He proposed an "Alliance for Progress" with the Latin Americans to implement programs to stimulate social and economic development. The Agency for International Development (AID) was formed to coordinate foreign aid.

President Kennedy believed that Fidel Castro, in Cuba, represented a threat to the stability of other Latin American nations. Therefore, he agreed to continue a project which was begun during the previous administration. A small army of anti-Castro Cuban exiles was trained in Central America. On April 17, 1961, it landed at the Bay of Pigs in Cuba, expecting American air support and help from the Cubans on the island. The invaders were quickly crushed and the entire mission collapsed when Kennedy withdrew air support.

Tensions with the Soviet Union continued. Tension worsened when the Americans discovered that the Soviets were constructing missile sites in Cuba. Most Americans believed this was an act of aggression. President Kennedy established a naval and air blockade around Cuba. Nevertheless, work on the missile sites continued. Preparations were being made for an American air attack on the missile sites. President Kennedy received a message from the Soviets that they would remove the missile bases in exchange for an American pledge not to invade Cuba. The president agreed and the crisis was over. More important, in 1963, Soviets and the Americans concluded a treaty to ban testing of nuclear weapons in the atmosphere.

The problems in Vietnam dominated the presidential office. The war began so slowly that few people knew why it started. By 1958 a civil war was being fought in Vietnam. Ho Chi Minh's Communist government was located in North Vietnam with its capital in Hanoi, and a pro-Western regime, under Ngo Dinh Diem, was located in South Vietnam with its capital in Saigon. President Kennedy decided to expand the American involvement when Diem was deposed by the South Vietnamese military leaders. President Johnson was advised that the United States had an obligation to resist communism in Vietnam. Congress had authorized the president to protect American forces and prevent further aggression in Southeast Asia. As American soldiers assumed an active role in the war, the casualties increased. Finally, a stable government was created in the South under General Nguyen Van Thieu. American forces were in Vietnam for seven years.

American involvement became more unpopular in the United States as more soldiers and resources were sent to Vietnam. In 1968 the president ordered a halt to American bombing of North Vietnam, and peace talks between the United States and North Vietnam began in Paris. Much of the anti-war feelings were directed against the president, and he decided not to seek another term. Some people felt it was a war that could not be won. Objections to the war emerged on university campuses as students organized peace marches and demonstrations. People began to raise questions about the wisdom and morality of the Vietnam War. Even U. S. allies began to criticize American involvement in Vietnam.

By the end of 1967, the protests against the war and the deteriorating racial situations helped to create deep social and political tension. During Tet, the Vietnamese lunar New Year, North Vietnam launched a campaign that attacked the United States Embassy in Saigon. This event destroyed all hope for victory in Vietnam and led to a change in American policy. This was a definite political defeat for the administration.

Eugene McCarthy of Wisconsin and Robert Kennedy of New York were two peace candidates for the Democratic presidential nomination. In the midst of this bitter political battle, Martin Luther King, Jr., was assassinated in Memphis, Tennessee. Robert Kennedy continued his campaign for the presidential nomination until he was assassinated in California in 1968. These were shattering experiences for the American people. When the Democrats met in Chicago, the police and protesters, opponents of war, clashed in a bloody riot in the streets of Chicago. Hubert Horatio Humphrey of Minnesota was nominated as the Democratic candidate for president. The Republican party nominated Richard Nixon. Nixon's presidential victory indicated that people were more interested in stability than in social change.

QUOTATIONS

Study the following quotations. For each one note—
        a. Who said the words?
        b. When was it said?
        c. Where was it said?
        d. Why was it said?
        e. What do you think the words meant when they were first spoken, and now, what
          do they mean to you? Explain.

A. "We dare not forget today that we are the heirs of that first revolution. Let the word go forth from this time and place, to friend and foe alike, that the torch has been passed to a new generation of Americans—born in this century tempered by war, disciplined by a hard and bitter peace, proud of our ancient heritage—and unwilling to witness or permit the slow undoing of those human rights to which this nation has always been committed, and to which we are committed today at home and around the world. Let every nation know, whether it wishes us well or ill, that we shall pay any price, bear any burden, meet any hardship, support any friend, oppose any foe to assume the survival and the success of liberty."

_____

_____

B. "I say to you today, my friends, that in spite of the difficulties and frustrations of the moment I still have a dream. It is a dream deeply rooted in the American dream.
I have a dream that one day this nation will rise up and live out the true meaning of its creed: 'We hold these truths to be self-evident; that all men are created equal.'
I have a dream that one day on the red hills of Georgia the sons of former slaves and the sons of former slave owners will be able to sit down together at the table of brotherhood."

_____

_____

C. "There is no Negro problem. There is no Southern problem. There is no Northern problem. There is only an American problem. And we are met here tonight as Americans, not as Democrats or Republicans, we are met here as Americans to solve that problem . . . .
Those words (from the Declaration of Independence) are a promise to every citizen that he shall share in the dignity of man. This dignity cannot be found in a man's possessions. It cannot be found in his power or in his position. It really rests on his right to be treated as a man equal in opportunity to all others. It says that he shall share in freedom, he shall choose his leaders, educate his children, provide for his family, according to his ability and his merits as a human being.
To apply another test—to deny a man his hopes because of his color or race, or his religion, or the place of his birth—is not only to do injustice, it is to deny America and to dishonor the dead who gave their lives for American freedom."

_____

_____

Name _____

DATES AND EVENTS

Tell what happened on each of the following dates. (This activity may be assigned as group work.)

1. January 20, 1961 _____

_____

2. September 22, 1961 _____

_____

3. June 25, 1962 _____

_____

4. August 28, 1963 _____

_____

5. November 22, 1963 _____

_____

6. January 23, 1964 _____

_____

7. January 4, 1965 _____

_____

8. August 11, 1965 _____

_____

9. March 16, 1966 _____

_____

10. August 20, 1967 _____

_____

11. April 4, 1968 _____

_____

12. January 20, 1969 _____

_____

SUGGESTED TEACHING ACTIVITIES

1. Topics for further study:
   - a. John F. Kennedy
   - b. Lyndon B. Johnson
   - c. "New Frontier"
   - d. "The Great Society"
   - e. Peace Corps
   - f. Head Start Program
   - g. James Meredith
   - h. "freedom rides"
   - i. Malcolm X
   - j. Fidel Castro
   - k. Robert Kennedy
   - l. student protest
   - m. affirmative action
   - n. Vietnam Conflict
   - o. Barry Goldwater
   - p. Hubert H. Humphrey
   - q. black power
   - r. race riots
   - s. Cuban Missile Crisis
   - t. Martin Luther King, Jr.

2. Imagine that you are the editor of your local newspaper; write an editorial concerning how you feel about American involvement in Vietnam, the Great Society, the peace marches, or the race riots.

3. As Afro-Americans, students, and sympathizers marched for the civil rights and peace movements, they sang many songs such as "We Shall Overcome." Folk singers, such as Joan Baez and Pete Seeger, featured these songs in their concerts. Student volunteers may plan a concert for their classmates which includes some of the popular songs of the civil rights and peace movements.

4. Assign students to interview a family member, neighbor, and/or friend who had one of the following experiences as a participant and/or witness (television, radio, newspapers) of any one of the following events: civil rights movement, student protest demonstration, race riots in the cities, assassination of President Kennedy, Robert Kennedy, or Martin Luther King, Jr. Have students share their findings with their classmates in a class discussion. Why are there different perceptions of the same experience?

5. Assign students to make a survey (include at least five people) reflecting how people felt on the day of the assassination of President Kennedy, Robert Kennedy, or Martin Luther King, Jr. Discuss what a survey is, how to formulate a question, how to approach an individual, and how to analyze and present findings.

6. On July 20, 1969, Neil Armstrong became the first man to set foot on the moon. Assign student volunteers to prepare a report on the space program during the 1960s and short biographical sketches of the astronauts who were selected to participate in the different launchings. A bulletin board display of the space program can be a part of the assignment.

7. Activism in government was evident in the Supreme Court under Chief Justice Earl Warren. Assign students to study the controversies and the decisions in each of the following cases and report their findings to their classmates: *Mapp v. Ohio* (1961), *Gideon v. Wainwright* (1963), *Engel v. Vitale* (1962), *Miranda v. Arizona* (1966), *Baker v. Carr* (1962).

8. As a class, view the video about the life of Mahatma Gandhi. How did Mahatma Gandhi's approach to solving problems influence Martin Luther King, Jr.? Discuss specific examples from the lives of these men indicating similarities and differences in their concepts of leadership and of achieving change. Discuss effectiveness of nonviolent techniques and terrorism in achieving social and political changes.

THE CRISIS IN THE PRESIDENCY

In electing Richard Nixon to the presidency in 1968, people wanted a more stable and secure existence, dedicated to traditional American values. Students, during the 1960s, formed various groups which appealed to many idealistic young Americans. Students for a Democratic Society was formed in Port Huron, Michigan, in 1962 to give students power to make political demands. Disputes on the Berkeley campus of the University of California involved the rights of students to engage in political activities on campus. Anti-war demonstrations were evident in many universities, making them a serious issue in American politics. Opposition to military conscription was also organized by student groups. Draft cards were burned, many draft-age Americans accepted long imprisonments, and others left the country.

Many young Americans were involved in the counterculture, a movement which challenged moral values and personal behavior of society. The most committed critics were known as the *hippies*. They rejected modern society and wanted to find life in a simple, more natural environment where they would seek personal fulfillment. They distinguished themselves from the rest of society by their hair style, dress, and music.

American Indians, or Native Americans, had been ignored for many years. They had many justifiable grievances against society. They lived on reservations where conditions were poor, opportunities limited, and many rights and privileges denied. In 1961 the Native Americans issued the Declaration of Indian Purpose which emphasized their right to choose their own way of life and their responsibility to preserve their heritage. In 1968 the American Indian Movement was established. In that same year, Congress passed the Indian Civil Rights Act which guaranteed the Bill of Rights to Indians living on reservations, and it also recognized the legality of tribal laws. In November 1972, about 1,000 Sioux Indian protesters occupied the building of the Bureau of Indian Affairs in Washington for six days. Another protest occurred at Wounded Knee, South Dakota, the site of the 1890 massacre of Sioux by federal troops. In 1970 the Sioux seized Wounded Knee and occupied it for two months, demanding changes in the administration of the reservation and insisting that government honor treaty obligations. The Native Americans presented lawsuits in court citing federal violation of treaty obligations.

The Hispanic Americans included a large number of Spanish-speaking people. Most of the Hispanic Americans were Mexican Americans with others coming from Cuba, Puerto Rico, Guatemala, and other countries in Latin America. Their living conditions were poor and they had little political influence until Cesar Chavez began organizing the farm workers. In California, Cesar Chavez created a union for migrant farm workers, the United Farm Workers. The members were mostly Hispanics. A strike was called in 1965 against the growers to demand recognition of the union and increased wages and benefits. When the growers resisted, he enlisted the aid of many other sympathetic organizations to help in boycotting grapes and lettuce. The grape growers finally signed contracts with the United Farm Workers.

Women, hardly a minority comprising 51 percent of the population, have changed their role more radically than any other group in society. Betty Friedan's book, *The Feminine Mystique*, made people more aware of discriminatory practices against women and urged women to demand equal rights.

Women were experiencing widespread discrimination in making career choices and in the workplace. President Kennedy's Commission on the Status of Women made people aware of sexual discrimination and created a network of women activists who worked for legislation. In the Civil Rights Act of 1964, it stated that discrimination based on a person's sex was illegal. In 1966 the National Organization for Women was organized. Women wanted greater educational opportunities and justice in the workplace. During the 1970s American women united with one another to force social change in their various roles such as wife, mother, and wage earner. In 1971 the government extended its affirmative action guidelines to include women. Major educational institutions opened their doors to women; women became an important force in business and in the professions.

When President Nixon assumed office, he was confronted with his promise to bring "peace with honor" in Vietnam. President Nixon appointed as his special assistant for national security affairs, Henry Kissinger. The demonstrations, prayer vigils, and picketing continued as a protest against the war in Vietnam. Many young people were unwilling to be drafted for a senseless war. A new system of military draft was devised. President Nixon and Henry Kissinger formulated a plan to train and equip the South Vietnamese military troops (instead of the American forces) to assume the responsibilities of combat. Beginning in 1969, American ground troops were slowly being withdrawn from Vietnam. President Nixon ordered an invasion of Cambodia and renewed the bombing of North Vietnam.

On May 4, four college students were killed and nine others injured when members of the National Guard opened fire on anti-war demonstrators at Kent State University in Ohio. Ten days later, two Afro-American students at Jackson State University in Mississippi were killed while demonstrating. It appeared that the war in Vietnam was becoming even more demanding. The negotiations for peace continued but agreements were too few. The peace talks broke off. Finally, on January 27, 1973, representatives of the United States, North and South Vietnam, and the provisional government in South Vietnam signed an agreement to end the war and restore peace in Vietnam. The agreement called for immediate cease fire, release of American prisoners of war, and American withdrawal of troops.

In February 1972, President Nixon visited the People's Republic of China. The United States government had not, even after 22 years, recognized the Chinese government. President Nixon announced that the United States would support Red China's membership in the United Nations and establish cultural ties with them. A few months later, President Nixon traveled to Moscow and signed the arms control agreement. In June 1973, Premier Leonid Brezhnev visited Washington, D. C. The Soviets and the Americans agreed not to become involved in a nuclear war. They also agreed to limit the production of nuclear weapons and to develop more cooperation between the two countries. President Nixon was successful in easing tensions and reducing the risks of war with Communist powers.

The Middle East was another trouble spot for the United States. On the evening of Yom Kippur in 1973, the holiest day in the Hebrew calendar, the Egyptian and Syrian forces attacked the Israelis by surprise. The Israelis suffered heavy losses. Within a couple of weeks, though, they were able to push back the enemies. The Soviets threatened to intervene. President Nixon ordered American military forces on alert. The Soviets backed down and agreed that the United Nations should establish a peacekeeping force in the region.

During President Nixon's administration, there were four vacancies on the Supreme Court. When Chief Justice Earl Warren retired in 1969, Warren P. Burger was appointed as Chief Justice. He did not believe that the federal courts should be involved in bringing about social or political change. President Nixon, later, appointed three other members to the Supreme Court. The Supreme Court, now, was not as active as it had been under Chief Justice Warren.

In the presidential election of 1972, President Nixon was renominated by the Republicans. The Democrats nominated Senator George S. McGovern of South Dakota, an outspoken opponent to the war in Vietnam, who was defeated by President Nixon.

The United States economy was rather stable except for the rising rate of inflation. By the late 1960s, the world economy had changed as it related to the United States. The United States did not have exclusive access to raw materials. Other nations were now competing for the same raw materials and sources of energy such as oil. A few nations controlled the world's oil supply and they could raise prices whenever they wished.

Public expectations of the presidency had increased since World War II. At the same time the controls on the authority of the presidency had also grown. President Nixon was rigid and authoritarian in his role as president. Early on the morning of June 17, 1972, the police caught five burglars who broke into the Democratic National Committee offices located in the Watergate office building in Washington, D. C. These burglars were Republicans and former employees of the president's reelection committee. One of them had worked in the White House. Supposedly, they had been paid for the burglary from a secret fund controlled by members of the White House staff. Early in 1973 the Watergate burglars went on trial. The trial and the investigations indicated that top presidential advisers were involved. Many of them were found guilty and sent to prison. There was never any conclusive evidence that the president had planned or approved of the burglary in advance. There was evidence, though, that President Nixon had tried to cover up the crime and to hinder its investigation. Congress recommended that President Nixon be impeached or brought to trial before the Senate. On August 8, 1974, President Nixon addressed the nation and announced his resignation. He was the first president of the United States ever to do so.

The vice president, Gerald Rudolph Ford of Michigan, became the thirty-eighth president of the United States. He was an honest and caring individual who enjoyed popularity until he pardoned former President Richard Nixon. He continued Nixon's foreign policies. The unemployment rates and inflation rates were increasing. In the 1976 presidential election, the Democratic candidate, Jimmy Carter of Georgia, was victorious.

MAKING CONNECTIONS

Explain in one or two sentences all of the ways in which Column I is connected to the corresponding item in Column II.

COLUMN I		COLUMN II
1. Cesar Chavez	_____	farm workers
2. Watergate investigations	_____	Gerald R. Ford
3. Betty Friedan	_____	National Organization for Women
4. President Nixon	_____	Henry Kissinger
5. anti-war demonstrations	_____	President Johnson
6. Chief Justice Earl Warren	_____	Warren P. Burger
7. President Richard Nixon	_____	John N. Mitchell
8. President Gerald Ford	_____	Nelson A. Rockefeller

MAP STUDY

On a map of Southeast Asia, locate the following places: North Vietnam, South Vietnam, Cambodia, Thailand, Laos, China, Saigon, Da Nang, Gulf of Tonkin, Hanoi, Dien Bien Phu, Phnom Penh, Mekong River, Haiphong, Vientiane, South China Sea.

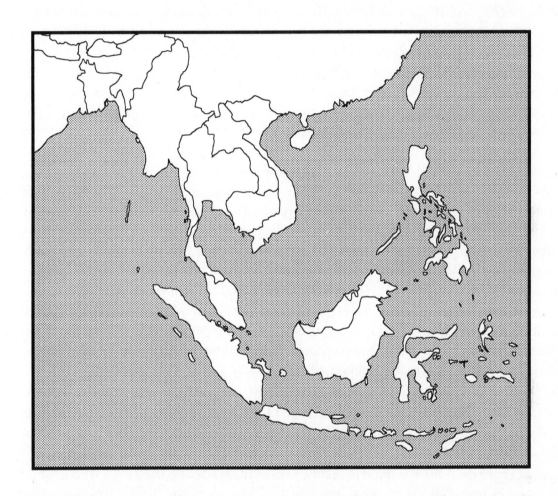

How do you think Americans felt when Vietnam, in 1975, became a single nation under a Communist government? Why?

_____
_____
_____
_____
_____
_____
_____
_____
_____

SUGGESTED TEACHING ACTIVITIES

1. Suggested topics for further study:
   - a. Richard Nixon
   - b. Cesar Chavez
   - c. Native Americans
   - d. Wounded Knee (1890 and 1970)
   - e. Hispanic Americans
   - f. Watergate burglary
   - g. Three Mile Island
   - h. Betty Friedan
   - i. arms limitation

2. Assign students to study the conditions of American Indians/Native Americans during the 1960s, 1970s, and 1980s and the legislation passed to help improve those conditions. What did the Native Americans demand from the government? Were they justified? Who were their leaders? List on the chalkboard the changes that occurred during that time period.

3. Read to the class the book entitled *Brother Eagle! Sister Sky—A Message From Chief Seattle*, paintings by Susan Jeffers (New York: Dial Books, 1991). Share the paintings with the class. This book makes a powerful statement about people and the environment, Native Americans, values, responsibilities, and conflict. What is its message to people of today? To people of the future?

4. During the 1970s and 1980s there was a great increase in the number of immigrants coming to the United States. Assign students to find out who came, from where, how many, why they came, and the problems, if any, that they experienced in their new country. Also, students might find out what kind of assistance is available if immigrants have difficulties in adjusting to their new home. Share the findings with the class. Students, in small groups or in one group, may develop a chart using the information that is collected.

5. Assign students to interview their grandmothers, neighbors, or friends to find out what changes have occurred in the role of women during their lifetime and how they feel about them and why. Some students may find it interesting to interview grandfathers, neighbors, or friends to find out how they feel about the changing role of women. Based upon the class discussion, the changes can be listed on the chalkboard.

6. In 1991 the percentage of persons in the population of the United States who were below the poverty level was 14.2%. Of that percentage 11.3% were white, 32.7% were Afro-Americans, and 28.7% were of Hispanic origin. Provide students with these statistics. Class Discussion: What do these percentages imply? Explain. Can poverty be eliminated? Explain.

7. Assign students to list the notable manned space flights during the 1970s, 1980s, and 1990s. Note the date, astronauts involved, purpose, and findings of the flights. How has society improved because of the space flight program?

8. Assign students to find out how much oil the United States produced and how much Americans consumed during the last 10 years. Then, assign students to prepare a list of the members of OPEC (Organization of Petroleum Exporting Countries). What is the purpose of this organization and why is the United States concerned about the Middle East? How does the United States show its concern? Are there other leading oil-producing nations which are not located in the Middle East? List the nations. What is the United States' relationship with these nations? How has the United States tried to solve problems that are caused by a shortage of oil?

9. Assign students to select at least 10 significant events, such as the Kent State University demonstration, the resignation of President Nixon, and others which occurred during the 1960s and 1970s and to prepare a time line.

PROGRESSING TOWARD A NEW CENTURY

President Jimmy Carter, former governor of Georgia, began his administration with several critical problems. He issued pardons to thousands of young men who had evaded the military draft during the Vietnam War. Unemployment rates declined as President Carter's economic program increased spending for public works and services and cut federal taxes. President Carter's proposed energy program to help eliminate or ease America's dependence on foreign oil imports depended heavily on energy conservation. Therefore, a Department of Energy was created.

When President Carter took office, he became a strong voice for human rights in foreign affairs. He completed talks on two treaties regarding the Panama Canal. The United States agreed to hand over the Canal to the government of Panama by the year 2000. The second treaty guaranteed the neutrality of the waterway to all shipping. The United States would have the right to defend the neutrality of the canal. The treaties were ratified.

President Carter was successful in arranging a peace treaty between President Anwar Sadat of Egypt and Prime Minister Menachem Begin of Israel. The problem about Jewish settlements in the disputed territory of the West Bank of the Jordan River was a troublesome one. Finally, President Sadat agreed to delay the issue of Palestinian refugees, and the treaty was signed between the two nations in 1979. Washington also announced, in 1979, the restoration of diplomatic relations between the United States and China.

The United States had provided political and military support to the government of the Shah of Iran. The Shah was a repressive and autocratic ruler. In January 1979, a revolutionary movement forced him to leave his country. The people had deep resentments toward him and the United States. On November 4, 1979, the Iranians invaded the American embassy in Teheran and seized the diplomats and military personnel inside and held them hostage for the return of the Shah to Iran in exchange for their freedom. The Shah was in a New York City hospital where he was being treated for cancer. The militants released a few of the hostages within a few days. However, 53 Americans remained prisoners in the embassy for over a year.

On December 17, 1979, the Soviet troops invaded Afghanistan. The United Nations asked the Soviets to withdraw, but they did not. During the political conventions of 1980, the Democrats again nominated Jimmy Carter and the Republicans nominated Ronald Reagan, a former California governor. Ronald Reagan won with an overwhelming majority of votes. On the day of President Reagan's inauguration, the remaining American hostages were released.

President Reagan promised the American people that he would restore the nation's military strength, reduce the influence of government in American life, and bring about a stable economy. His approach to the economy was known as "supply-side" economics. He reduced taxes on corporations and wealthy individuals to encourage new investments. Since these tax cuts would reduce government revenues, it would also be necessary to reduce government expenses. There was a drastic cut in the federal budget. Unemployment was increasing. The federal debt under President Reagan increased dramatically. An imbalance in American trade was noticeable. By the middle

1980s the United States had become the world's largest debtor. The 1981 tax cuts and the increase in military spending did not help to stabilize the economy. President Reagan refused to raise income taxes to reduce the deficit. He made budget cuts in programs which serviced the needy and poor such as reductions in funding for food stamps, decreasing federal subsidies for low-income housing, limitations on Medicare and Medicaid payments, reductions in student loans, school lunches, and other educational programs. Congress passed legislation which would set budget goals that would reduce the deficit each year until a balanced budget was achieved.

President Reagan believed that the United States should be active and assertive in opposing communism throughout the world and in supporting friendly governments. U.S. relations with the Soviet Union were becoming worse. The Strategic Defense Initiative (SDI), known as Star Wars, claimed that a system could be built that would intercept and destroy nuclear missiles fired at the United States, making nuclear war obsolete. The Soviets were angry and alarmed.

In October 1983, American soldiers and marines were sent to the island of Grenada in the Caribbean to oust an anti-American government that was friendly with the Soviet Union. President Reagan's firm policy against Soviet expansion extended into Central America. He sent military advisers to El Salvador where guerrilla tactics and Soviet influence were evident. Confrontations between the United States and the Soviet-supported groups continued in El Salvador and Nicaragua. The Reagan administration gave material support to the "contras," a guerrilla movement, whose objective was to overthrow the Sandinista government in Nicaragua.

In the Middle East, in June 1982, the Israeli Army invaded Lebanon to drive out Palestinian guerrillas from the country. An American peacekeeping force entered Beirut to supervise the withdrawal of Palestinian forces. American marines remained in the city to protect the Lebanese government which was involved in a civil war. In 1983 a terrorist bombing of the marine barracks in Beirut left over 200 Americans dead. This bombing made Americans more aware of the use of terrorism by groups to achieve their political objectives. To punish terrorism, President Reagan ordered American planes to bomb the capital of Libya because he believed that their leader encouraged terrorism.

At the Democratic Convention of 1984 in San Francisco, the Democrats nominated Walter Mondale for the presidency and selected the first female candidate for the vice presidency, Representative Geraldine Ferraro of New York. President Reagan's popularity with the American public was impressive as was his victory against Walter Mondale.

There was a series of scandals during President Reagan's administration. Many of his top officials resigned from office. One scandal involved the misuse of funds by the Department of Housing and Urban Development. Another scandal involved the savings and loan industry. The government had sharply reduced its regulatory controls over the savings and loan companies. Through reckless expansion and speculation and with personal corruption, industry was in chaos. The government was forced to step in to prevent a complete collapse. The eventual cost to taxpayers of rescuing the banks ran as high as five hundred billion dollars.

The White House conceded that it had entered into secret negotiations with the revolutionary government of Iran to secure the release of several Americans being held hostage by radical Islamic groups in the Middle East. This contradicted the president's promise that he would never negotiate with terrorists. The United States was selling arms to Iran in exchange for assistance. Some of the money from the arms deal with Iran had been used to aid the contras in Nicaragua. Marine Lieutenant Colonel Oliver North, assigned to the staff of the National Security Council, admitted ignoring the law and insisted that he had the right to do so and that he was following the orders of his superiors.

Many people were alarmed that President Reagan was not attending to serious social problems such as poverty, homelessness, drugs, and education. In the presidential election of 1988, the Democrats nominated the governor of Massachusetts, Michael Dukakis, with Lloyd Bentsen, senator from Texas, as his running mate. George Bush was nominated by the Republicans, and

Senator J. Danforth Quayle of Indiana became his choice of a vice presidential running mate. George Bush defeated Michael Dukakis.

President Bush gave speeches supporting education, the environment, and other pressing social problems. However, no funding was appropriated for these programs. President Bush sent American troops to Panama in 1989 to overthrow the unpopular military leader, Manuel Noriega, and established an elected pro-American government in Panama.

Mikhail Gorbachev, leader of Soviet Union, was a revolutionary figure who changed his nation by introducing two policies. One policy, *Glasnost*, introduced personal and political liberties to Soviet life. The other, *Perestroika*, attempted to introduce private ownership and the profit motive into the Soviet economy. The drastic change in the economy brought about shortages in food and consumer goods and the collapse of the Soviet empire. Nations under Soviet influence either overthrew their governments or forced them to create independent ones. The most dramatic moment was the dismantling of the Berlin Wall and, within a year, the reunification of Germany. By 1992 every nation within the Soviet Union had declared independence. Boris Yeltsin was elected the president of Russia, and Mikhail Gorbachev resigned as president of the U. S. S. R. which no longer existed. The Soviet threat had been removed.

On August 2, 1990, Saddam Hussein, leader of Iraq, invaded Kuwait and announced that it was now Iraqi territory. The United States and its allies sent military forces along the border between Kuwait and Saudi Arabia. By late 1990, the Bush administration began to prepare for war. On January 12, Congress voted to authorize the use of force against Iraq. On January 16, American and allied air forces began bombardment of Iraqi forces in Kuwait and of military and industrial installations in Iraq itself. Under the command of General Norman Schwarzkopf, American ground troops were used in the Gulf War. On February 28, Iraqi officials announced acceptance of allied terms for cease fire. The Gulf War came to an end. Kuwait was restored to its former rulers and Saddam Hussein survived.

During the Bush administration, a civil rights bill to combat job discrimination was enacted. Many large corporations declared bankruptcy. The cost of health care was rising. As the economy began to falter in the early 1990s, many Americans began to feel that the administration was not active enough in trying to find solutions. Bill Clinton, governor of Arkansas, was victorious over incumbent President George Bush and independent candidate Ross Perot in the presidential election of 1992.

President Clinton's budget package was passed in Congress. His cabinet appointments reflected the cultural, sexual, and racial diversity of our nation. The American public approved of his leadership during the natural disasters such as floods and earthquakes. He has been confronted with many issues such as homosexuals in the armed forces, welfare reform, and in foreign affairs with problems in Somalia, Haiti, North Korea, and Herzegovina and Bosnia. Hillary Rodham Clinton, his wife, headed a task force which developed a proposal for a health care program. He has found himself in difficult and embarrassing personal and public situations. It still remains to be seen how effective President Clinton will be as he continues to work on domestic and foreign policies during his administration. There are no easy answers to the many problems challenging American society. Even as some of the problems are solved, new problems arise. Responsible and visionary leaders are needed to help improve life for all Americans.

PREDICTING THE FUTURE

Read the following predictions. Then, tell whether you think it will happen or will not happen by indicating *yes* or *no*.

_____ 1. The life expectancy of Americans will increase in the next decade.

_____ 2. The Republicans will win the presidential election of 1996.

_____ 3. The number of families who are homeless will increase.

_____ 4. The unemployment rate will continue to increase in the next decade.

_____ 5. By 2050 the population of the United States will include a majority of people representing Hispanic, Asian, and Afro-American groups rather than people of European heritage.

_____ 6. Universal health care will be a benefit of citizenship in the United States.

_____ 7. The gap between those who have (wealthy) and those who do not have (poor) will widen.

_____ 8. By 2050 the planet Earth will not be able to provide for the exploding population.

_____ 9. By 2050 the United States will have found a substitute form of energy and will not be dependent upon the Middle East for oil.

_____ 10. Air pollution will be eliminated in America's large cities.

_____ 11. More people will own helicopters than automobiles by 2050.

_____ 12. Public transportation will be used more than private transportation.

_____ 13. The number of crimes committed in the United States will decrease.

_____ 14. Most of the people in the United States will be employed in service occupations rather than in heavy industry.

_____ 15. The information superhighway will almost make libraries and shopping malls obsolete.

_____ 16. Within five years people will be carrying portable telephones in their pockets or purses.

_____ 17. A woman will be elected president of the United States in 2010.

_____ 18. More people will be living in apartments or condominiums than in family homes.

_____ 19. The American economy will have a difficult time keeping up with world competitors.

_____ 20. Machines, or robots, will be able to make independent, low-level decisions.

_____ 21. Tourists will be purchasing travel packages to the moon by 2075.

SUGGESTED TEACHING ACTIVITIES

1. Topics for further study:
   a. human rights
   b. Panama Canal
   c. President Anwar Sadat
   d. welfare reform
   e. Star Wars
   f. Haiti
   g. Somalia
   h. William J. Clinton
   i. Hillary R. Clinton
   j. health care plan
   k. Mikhail S. Gorbachev
   l. George Bush

2. Using the activity (page 120) entitled "Predicting the Future," survey the class on each prediction and then discuss the reasons why students believe each prediction will or will not happen. Also, assign students to make predictions of their own and share them with the class.

3. Assign students to write a short report on the Iran Hostage Crisis. The report should include the following information: Who was involved? How many hostages were taken? Where did it occur? When did it occur? Why did it occur? How long were they held hostage? How was the situation finally resolved? Optional: What were the experiences of some of the hostages during their 444 days of confinement?

4. Assign students to respond to the following questions and to give reasons for their choices.

   a. If you were a voter in 1976, would you have voted for Jimmy Carter or Gerald R. Ford?
   b. If you were a voter in 1980, would you have voted for Jimmy Carter, Ronald Reagan, John B. Anderson, or Ed Clark?
   c. If you were a voter in 1988, would you have voted for George Bush or Michael S. Dukakis?
   d. What factors did you consider when you made your decision? Explain.

5. Ask students to consider and discuss the following situations:

   a. What would have happened if President Carter had been successful in freeing the hostages in Iran?
   b. What would have happened if the Gulf War had lasted for at least a year?

6. Assign student volunteers to present a special report on the Gulf War. Why was the United States involved? What countries and personalities were involved in this war? What military strategies were used? How effective were they? Who emerged as heroes of this war? What did the United States gain in participating in this war? What role was played by the communication media? A map of the area would be helpful as students present the report.

7. Map Study: Assign students to study a map of the world published in 1960 and one published recently. Prepare a list of at least five changes on the map and note the reasons for the changes.

8. Assign students to write a composition entitled "The One Memorable Incident in United States History" and/or "The One Outstanding Individual in United States History."

Answer Key

CHANGE AND DISCORD BEFORE THE CIVIL WAR

Identifying Major Events   Page 3

1. 1850: A set of resolutions presented to Congress to end the dispute over the slavery issue. It admitted California as a free state; the lands of New Mexico and Utah were to be divided into territories and the settlers would decide whether it would or would not be a slave state; slave trade would end in District of Columbia; and a stronger fugitive slave law was included. The stricter fugitive slave law angered many Northerners who resisted its enforcement.

2. 1851: This novel portrayed slaves as human beings and it caused many people to oppose slavery.

3. 1854: This act divided the Louisiana Territory into Kansas and Nebraska Territories; to be a slave or free state would be determined by vote by its people. This led to many protest meetings, the formation of the Republican Party, and eventually to violence as the South and North tried to populate the state with people who would vote their way.

4. 1857: The decision ruled that Dred Scott, a slave, was property with no rights as a citizen or person. Too, slavery could not be legally banned from the territories. The South approved of the decision but in the North it was denounced. The Democratic Party was weakened because the Southern Democrats favored the decision.

5. 1858: These debates were held when Douglas and Lincoln competed for the Illinois Senate seat. Douglas believed in popular sovereignty, that is, the people, not Congress, had the right to determine whether their state was to be free or slave. Lincoln opposed this view. Lincoln lost the election. The debates made Lincoln a national figure and helped him gain the Republican nomination for president in 1860.

6. 1859: John Brown, an abolitionist, raided Harpers Ferry to get guns to use in a revolt against slave owners. He was caught, found guilty of murder and treason, and was hanged. Now, many people believed that only through a war would slaves be freed.

7. 1860: Lincoln was elected president. There was no longer any hope for compromise between North and South. Lincoln did not support the idea that states could break away from the Union when they wished. His party also wanted to do away with all slavery; slavery should be kept out of the new territories.

Map Study   Page 4

Free States: Pennsylvania, New Jersey, Connecticut, Massachusetts, New Hampshire, New York, Rhode Island, Vermont, Kentucky, Ohio, Indiana, Illinois, Maine, Michigan, Iowa, Wisconsin, California, Minnesota, and Oregon.

Slave States: Alabama, Florida, Georgia, Louisiana, Mississippi, South Carolina, Texas, Virginia, Arkansas, North Carolina, Tennessee, West Virginia, Delaware, Maryland, and Missouri.

1. The voters of New Mexico and Utah would decide to be either a free or a slave state.

2. The voters in the Kansas and Nebraska territories would decide whether they should be a free or slave state.

THE INEVITABLE WAR OF REBELLION

The Matching Game   Page 8

1. b	5. f	9. d
2. c	6. a	10. e
3. j	7. k	11. l
4. h	8. i	12. g

Commanders of the North and South   Page 9

Responses will vary.

PEACEMAKING PROBLEMS AFTER THE CIVIL WAR

Making Connections   Page 14

1. f	6. k	11. c
2. l	7. i	12. m
3. b	8. n	13. g
4. e	9. a	14. d
5. h	10. j	

"Iffy" Questions   Page 15

1. Responses will vary.
2. Responses will vary.
3. Responses will vary.

RECONSTRUCTION COMES TO AN END

Getting the "Scoop"   Page 20

Responses will vary.

"Jim Crow" Laws   Page 21

1. The purposes were to prevent blacks from voting, to discriminate against blacks, and to keep blacks from achieving success politically, educationally, or economically.

2. Responses will vary.

3. The persons affected by the laws were blacks and poor whites. They did not have the organization for opposing the laws. They were denied education and were in constant fear of being terrorized by the Ku Klux Klan or lynched by mobs.

4. Responses will vary.

THE SOUTH AND CLOSING THE WESTERN FRONTIER

Putting Things in Order!   Page 26

Set I:	Set II:	Set III:
A. 2	A. 4	A. 2
B. 1	B. 2	B. 4
C. 4	C. 3	C. 3
D. 3	D 1	D 1

Set IV:	Set V:	Set VI:
A. 2	A. 3	A. 1
B. 1	B. 4	B. 2
C. 4	C. 1	C. 4
D. 3	D. 2	D. 3

Hunters of the Plains   Page 27

Responses will vary.

EXPANSION INTO AN INDUSTRIAL ECONOMY

Connecting People and Ideas   Page 32

1. k	8. q	15. d
2. h	9. o	16. r
3. j	10. s	17. n
4. l	11. f	18. p
5. b	12. t	19. g
6. i	13. a	20. m
7. e	14. u	21. c

Creating a Bar Graph   Page 33

1. The rise began in the 1880s and continued steadily. Industrialization was taking place. More technologies were developing and creating factory jobs and other jobs in the cities to provide services for people. Farmers were beginning to use more machinery on their farms; they needed fewer farmhands.

2. The sharpest increase was between 1900 and 1910. Immigration from Europe and more jobs in factories and stores to provide services for people in the cities contributed to this increase.

3. Responses will vary.

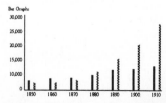

LIFE IN AMERICAN CITIES

The Art Gallery — **Page 37**
Selection One and Selection Two—Responses will vary.

The Big Cities — **Page 38**
1. It was the center of a vast transportation network. Train stations led to many other places, and port was available for ships. Men were willing to invest in buildings, going upward. It was near other large cities and farmlands. It is an exciting and dynamic city with many consumers. Offices and factories were located in the city. There was a massive communications system in the city.
2. Chicago grew very rapidly. Trains brought cattle and other products from the West to Chicago for meat packing. Other foodstuffs were brought to Chicago from the South and West—grains, corn, wheat, etc. It is located on Lake Michigan. Water transportation could be used on the Great Lakes.
3. Transportation and communication were important factors, by train or by water. Also, location of raw materials near the city was an important factor.
4. 1. New York: 7,322,564
   2. Los Angeles: 3,485,398
   3. Chicago: 2,783,726
   4. Houston: 1,630,553
   5. Philadelphia: 1,585,577
   6. San Diego: 1,110,549
   7. Detroit: 1,027,974
   8. Dallas: 1,006,877
   9. Phoenix: 983,403
   10. San Antonio: 935,933
5. Responses will vary.

HARD TIMES AND POLITICS IN AMERICA

Connecting Words and Definitions — **Page 43**
1. c   5. b   9. k   13. o
2. d   6. g   10. e   14. l
3. p   7. f   11. h   15. m
4. a   8. j   12. n   16. i

Presidential Elections — **Page 44**
1. Republican
2. 1876
3. Samuel J. Tilden received the majority of the popular vote but not the majority of electoral votes; therefore, he lost to President Hayes. Grover Cleveland also received the majority of the popular vote but not the majority of electoral votes; therefore, he lost to President Harrison.
4. He was an extremely powerful or strong candidate, a good campaigner. He received a good percentage of the votes although he did lose the election.
5. The population increased and the number in Congress for each state increased.

BECOMING A WORLD POWER

Map Study — **Page 49**
Student maps will vary in appearance.

If You Had Been . . . — **Page 50**
1. Responses will vary.
2. Responses will vary.
3. Responses will vary.

THE PROGRESSIVE MOVEMENT

Making Connections — **Page 55**
1. *The Jungle* was a novel about the workers in the stockyards, and it described how rotten meat was packed for sale. Shortly after Upton Sinclair published his book the Pure Food and Drug Act, which forbade the manufacture and sale of impure foods, drugs, and liquors, and the Meat Inspection Act were passed. The Inspection Act helped to eliminate many diseases that were transmitted by impure meat.
2. Jane Addams, a college graduate, established a settlement house, Hull House, in a poor Chicago neighborhood to help the needy and immigrants.
3. The Salvation Army was first founded in England and then established in the United States. The organization promoted the Christian faith and also provided for the needs of the poor living in cities.
4. Thomas L. Johnson was the reform mayor of Cleveland. He fought the powerful streetcar interests in Cleveland and eventually achieved city ownership of certain basic utilities.
5. Suffragists were reformers who worked to secure voting rights for women. Eventually, they were able to get Congress and the states to ratify the Nineteenth Amendment, giving women the right to vote.
6. The muckrakers were journalists and writers, such as Lincoln Steffens. He wrote articles, *The Shame of the Cities*, which exposed the corruption in cities and incited progressives to bring about changes in city government.
7. Tammany Hall, a powerful political machine, used its influence to pass legislation to eliminate tragedies such as the one that occurred at the Triangle Shirtwaist Factory. Through their support, strict regulations on factory owners and enforcement of those regulations to prevent fires were enacted.
8. Robert LaFollette was a leader in the progressive movement and governor of Wisconsin. He established many reforms in Wisconsin, such as curbing the power of interest groups.

What Does It Mean? — **Page 56**
1. e   5. h   9. b
2. f   6. d   10. c
3. i   7. k   11. a
4. j   8. g

ENTERING THE TWENTIETH CENTURY

Figuring Out Chronology — **Page 61**
1. (F) c   4. (F) c   7. (F) b
   (L) b   (L) b   (L) a

2. (F) c   5. (F) a   8. (F) a
   (L) a   (L) b   (L) c

3. (F) b   6. (F) c
   (L) c   (L) b

What Would You Have Done? — **Page 62**
Responses will vary.

THE "WAR TO END WARS"

Connecting Words and Definitions — **Page 67**
1. e   6. b
2. a   7. d
3. h   8. j
4. i   9. f
5. g   10. c

Life Can Be Exciting! — **Page 68**
Responses will vary.

AGE OF PROSPERITY AND CHANGE

The Arts in the 1920s — **Page 73**
Responses will vary.

The Automobile Changes American Life — **Page 74**
Responses will vary.

THE GREAT DEPRESSION

Finding Connections — **Page 78**
1. e   5. g   9. m
2. h   6. b   10. d
3. i   7. f   11. l
4. j   8. k   12. a
                    13. c

Unemployment Page 79
Bar Graph

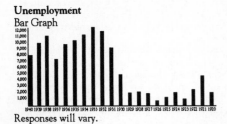

Responses will vary.

THE NEW DEAL

New Deal Legislation Page 84
1. To help farmers raise their income and to control the production of crops (reduce) to bring prices down. The processing tax from which farmers were paid to limit production was not a tax at all; therefore, the Supreme Court declared the AAA unconstitutional.
2. To develop the resources in the valley, to control flooding.
3. To provide inexpensive electrical power to people in isolated areas.
4. To list practices for fair competition and to give labor the right to collective bargaining. It was declared unconstitutional because it gave legislative powers to the president, and some of the industry codes covered business that took place entirely within a state.
5. To provide jobs for young men on various conservation projects.
6. To provide federal jobs.
7. To provide jobs in public works which would increase the buying power of workers.
8. To provide even more jobs in all areas of public works, arts, etc.
9. To provide job training and part-time jobs for needy students.
10. To provide pensions for retired workers and to aid the handicapped.
11. To define unfair labor practices and to establish the National Labor Relations Board.

People Are Important Page 85
1. e   5. k   9. c
2. i   6. j   10. g
3. d   7. b   11. a
4. f   8. h

AMERICA FACES A GLOBAL CRISIS

The Thirty-second President: FDR Page 90
Responses will vary.
Which Event Happened First? Page 91
1. b   5. a   9. a
2. b   6. a   10. c
3. a   7. b   11. a
4. b   8. b   12. c

THE COLD WAR

Presidential Elections Page 96
1. He was reluctantly elected as the Democratic candidate for the presidency. He was unable to get the cooperation of Congress to pass his legislation. His party was split and he was also unpopular.
2. Responses will vary
3. Responses will vary.
4. Responses will vary.

Making Connections With Terms and Meanings Page 97
1. f   6. j   11. k
2. l   7. m   12. e
3. n   8. a   13. h
4. c   9. d   14. b
5. i   10. g

PROSPERITY AND THE AMERICAN SOCIETY

Labor Force Page 102
1. Responses will vary.
2. More effective fertilizers and better irrigation techniques were available.

3. In 1880 mechanization of farm tasks and the growth of cities with jobs in industry took place.
4. Responses will vary. Nonfarm will continue to increase and farm to decrease.

"Iffy" Questions Page 103
Responses will vary.

HOPES AND FRUSTRATIONS OF THE SIXTIES

Quotations Page 108
A. John Fitzgerald Kennedy, January 20, 1961, Washington, D. C., during his inauguration as the thirty-fifth president of the United States. He spoke about the United States and its relationship with the rest of the world. Responses will vary.
B. Martin Luther King, Jr., August 28, 1963, in Washington, D. C., before the Lincoln Memorial to the "Freedom Marchers." This is a memorable address presented in the cadences of the black churches. Responses will vary.
C. Lyndon B. Johnson, March 15, 1965, on television as he addressed Congress to support the Voting Rights Act which would ensure Afro-Americans that they would not be kept from the poll. Responses will vary.

Dates and Events Page 109
1. John F. Kennedy is inaugurated as the thirty-fifth president of the United States.
2. Congress establishes the Peace Corps.
3. The Supreme Court rules that reading of prayers in New York public schools is unconstitutional.
4. Martin Luther King, Jr., makes his "I have a dream" speech during the March on Washington.
5. JFK is assassinated and LBJ is sworn in as president.
6. The Twenty-fourth Amendment is ratified, eliminating the poll tax in federal elections.
7. President Johnson presents his plan for the "Great Society" (State of the Union message).
8. Major race riot in Watts district of Los Angeles.
9. *Gemini 8*—first spacecraft to dock in space.
10. Thurgood Marshall is appointed as the first black justice to the Supreme Court.
11. Martin Luther King, Jr., is assassinated.
12. Richard M. Nixon is inaugurated as the thirty-seventh president of the United States.

THE CRISIS IN THE PRESIDENCY

Making Connections Page 114
1. Chavez organized the United Farm Workers, mostly Hispanics, and got growers to increase wages and benefits.
2. As a consequence of the Watergate scandal, Gerald Ford became president of the United States.
3. Betty Friedan's book made people aware of the treatment of women in society; this led to the organization of NOW as a vehicle to bring about change.
4. President Nixon relied heavily on Henry Kissinger as special adviser and secretary of state.
5. Anti-war demonstrations caused President Johnson not to seek reelection and historians to view his decision not to run as a failure.
6. Chief Justice Warren, an activist, was replaced by Warren Burger on the Supreme Court.
7. John N. Mitchell was President Nixon's attorney general and was involved in the Watergate scandal.
8. Rockefeller served as President Ford's vice president.

Map Study Page 115
Responses will vary.

PROGRESSING TOWARD A NEW CENTURY

Predicting the Future Page 120
Responses will vary.